W9-BVY-256

REINVENTING CHILDHOOD

Raising and Educating
Children in a Changing World

DAVID ELKIND

Modern Learning Press, Inc.
Rosemont, NJ

Publisher's Cataloging-in-Publication

Elkind, David, 1931-.
    Reinventing childhood: raising and educating children in
a changing world / by David Elkind. -- 1st ed.
      p. cm.
      Includes bibliographical references and index.
      ISBN: 1-56762-069-8

      1. Children--History. 2. Children--Sociological aspects.
3. Family--History. I. Title.

HQ767.87E55 1998   305.23′09
                         QBI97-41637

To the directors, teachers, and children of the Eliot Pearson Children's School and the Tufts Educational Day Care Center. They provide vital examples of how childhood can be reinvented to support both developmentally and individually appropriate practices.

Acknowledgments

There are so many people to whom I owe thanks. First of all, I owe a tremendous debt to those children, parents, teachers, and administrators whom I have had the good fortune to meet and talk with in the course of traveling and lecturing around the country. They have helped me to appreciate that while broad generalizations are important, so too are practical suggestions about what can be done in particular situations, both at home and at school. They have thus forced me to reinvent my own conception of childhood to include the vicissitudes of everyday life.

Next, I want to thank Bert Shapiro and Robert Low for encouraging me to write this book, and for the continued support and reassurance they and the new publisher of Modern Learning Press have provided along the way. I owe a special debt to Robert Low, who not only helped shape the book but whose careful and thoughtful editing have made it much more accessible and readable.

Finally, I want to thank my wife Debbie, my sons Paul, Robert, and Rick, and my new daughter-in-law Norma. They have, with this book and with previous ones, been extraordinarily gracious and forbearing in putting up with my preoccupations and obsessions. Writing is such a solitary activity, I am so very fortunate to have this wonderful "social capital" to support my scribbling.

East Sandwich, Massachusetts
1998

Contents

Preface i

Chapter 1
Inventing and Reinventing Childhood 1

Chapter 2
Modern Inventors of Childhood 19

Chapter 3
Reinventing Language Development 43

Chapter 4
Reinventing Socialization 63

Chapter 5
Reinventing Personality 87

Chapter 6
Reinventing Intelligence and Giftedness 111

Chapter 7
Reinventing Normality 131

Chapter 8
The Ongoing Process of
    Reinventing Childhood 153

Afterword
Reinventing Developmentally
    Appropriate Practice 173

Preface

I would like to begin this book by explaining it in relation to my earlier work and that of a few other authors. In the early 1980s, several books (e.g., Winn's *Children Without Childhood* and Postman's *The Disappearance of Childhood*) argued that childhood, as we once knew it, is disappearing. In my own book of that period, *The Hurried Child*, I did not agree that childhood was disappearing, only that children were being hurried through it too quickly. In my subsequent books, *Miseducation* and *All Grown Up and No Place to Go*, I further detailed this argument with respect to preschool children and adolescents. Hurrying young people at each of these stages of development, in my opinion, was stressful and unhealthy in many respects.

In a more recent book, *Ties That Stress*, I attempted to provide a broader context for this pressure on children and youth to grow up fast. I tried to show how it reflected the monumental changes in society and in the family during the past few decades. Briefly put, my thesis was that during the "modern" era, perhaps best represented by 1950s America, children's needs took precedence over those of adults, whereas now, in the "postmodern" era, the needs of adults tend to take precedence over those of children. It is in the context of this new "need imbalance," which results in children feeling that their needs are not being met, that we can understand the upsurge of problematic behavior among young people.

In all of these books, therefore, I have catalogued the negative consequences of our transition into a postmodern society. I still hold to those convictions, because the data on the problems of postmodern children is truly overwhelming. Nonetheless, it must be admitted that there have been many positive consequences of this change, as well. Perhaps the most significant result is the new recognition of the range of differences among children of the same age. During the modern era, to a large extent, the conception of childhood was predicated upon the differences *between* age groups and all but ignored the variability *within* them. It is only in the past few decades, for example, that we have begun to acknowledge and respond to the needs of bilingual and multilingual children, of children with disabilities, and of children with different learning styles and temperaments. In effect, the postmodern ethos has led to a "reinvention" of childhood that encompasses this diversity.

A prime example of these changes can be found in the books young children read during their first years of school, when they are learning about their world and themselves. During the 1950s, many American children read "basal readers" featuring Dick, Jane, and their friends, who were all white, attractive, and living in middle-class suburbs. There were no children of color, none who had special needs, and none who came from single-parent or remarried families. This narrowly conceived world carefully excluded any children or families that deviated from the ideal.

In contrast, today's classrooms usually include a variety of books that more accurately reflect the diversity of our society. Young children read about children whose skin color, family, country of origin, and specific needs are very different from their own. For better or worse, these same young children may also read books designed to help them understand and cope with divorce, illegal drugs, "good and bad touches," and other matters that would not have been considered appropriate reading material for young children during the modern era.

Clearly, this sort of change can have a profound impact on children. It also shows how the concept of childhood varies widely in different times and places. Yet, an important distinction is that the children themselves remain much the same in regard to their biological and developmental processes; what varies is the society and its effects on children, as well as the way in which children and their experiences are perceived.

Although specific aspects of the new postmodern conception of childhood have been presented in numerous articles and books dealing with topics such as multiculturalism or special needs, an inclusive presentation of this reinvention of childhood has not yet appeared. In part, this is a result of the fact that the re-invention of childhood is an ongoing process, rather than a one-time event. Some of the changes appear unrelated at first, and some are so gradual they can be difficult to detect. However, I believe that enough of this reinvention has now been accomplished to justify an attempt at presenting this change as a whole.

Accordingly, my main goal in this book is to provide a comprehensive overview of the postmodern reinvention of childhood. To put the presentation in context, some historical perspective is required, and this material is presented in the first section. An introductory chapter tells the story of our transition from a modern to a postmodern society, with particular attention paid to the transformation of the American family. A second chapter then offers a brief biographical sketch of the major crafters of modern childhood and a summary of their major theoretical contributions. In each case, the implications of their work for our postmodern times are also considered.

The next section is made up of five chapters that explore the reinvention of childhood in regard to domains such as language, intelligence, and personality. A final, concluding section examines some of the ongoing attempts at reinvention and the lessons to be learned from these efforts. An Afterword presents a few last thoughts on the postmodern reinvention of childhood.

To make this undertaking manageable, I have focused this material on the early childhood years, which are often defined as ages 4 through 8. Although the narratives of the reinvention of childhood and adolescence are in many ways parallel, there are also important differences. The story of the reinvention of childhood, like that of adolescence, therefore requires its own full-length treatment. Nonetheless, because there are areas that overlap, I do believe that some of the ideas offered here have relevance for parents and teachers of young people at all age levels.

Chapter 1

Inventing and Reinventing Childhood

The child is a gift of nature, but childhood is a social invention. How children are perceived, as opposed to how they are conceived, always reflects a social consensus. The novel idea that childhood is and should be fundamentally different from adulthood — and not just a more limited version of grown-up life — was first introduced to the Western world in the seventeenth century, when children were, for the first time, portrayed as something other than miniature adults.

The modern invention of childhood necessarily mirrored the basic assumptions and beliefs of that historical epoch. Now that we have moved — roughly since mid-century — into a postmodern era, we are reinventing childhood to reflect our contemporary perspectives and circumstances. To briefly summarize and contrast these visions of childhood, modern childhood was an abstract ideal based on norms of behavior, while postmodern childhood is a diverse collection of individualized portraits.

This chapter will explain how we were brought to this reinvention of childhood. It will also tell the story of the reinvention of the modern nuclear family as the postmodern "permeable" family. This additional narrative is needed because the family serves as the medium through which the societal conception of childhood is translated into specific child-rearing and educational practices.

When considering these changes, it is important to remember that social invention and reinvention are ongoing processes, not one-time events. Although I will present the different types

1

of childhoods and families in contrast to one another, they actually may overlap and merge in certain respects and circumstances.

The Modern World View

Many modern ideas can be traced to the eighteenth century period known as the Enlightenment. The spirit of the Enlightenment was that of free and unbridled inquiry and experimentation in the sciences and the arts. The modern world view encompassed a belief in the power of reason to solve all human problems and to advance the well-being of the whole of humankind. And, finally, it celebrated the significance and value of each individual's needs, talents, and abilities. With the Enlightenment, the authority of the Throne and of the Church was replaced by the authority of nature and of the common man and woman participating in a democracy.

The modern world view was based on three assumptions that were taken as fundamental and incontestable truths. The first of these was the belief in human *progress*. Thanks to rational science, it was believed, knowledge of the natural and physical world would accumulate and allow us to understand and control the world around us. A second fundamental modern tenet was that of *universality*. According to this belief, scientific research and reason would enable us to discover the universal laws that governed the natural world, as well as the universal social laws that regulated all human behavior. Finally, there was the belief in *regularity*. The conviction that underlying principles extended throughout the universe led to the treatment of any seeming irregularity as reflecting merely a gap in our knowledge.

Science exemplified these truths. Newton's laws of gravitation, for example, represented a notable advance over earlier astronomical theories. The laws of gravitation were also universal and held for objects on earth as well as those in our solar system.

And these laws were regular in that there were no exceptions to them. Likewise, in the nineteenth century, Darwin's theory of evolution progressed beyond earlier ideas of creationism. His principles of variation and natural selection were regarded as universal and as applicable to the human species as they were to the evolution of plants and animals. Later, Mendelian genetics revealed the genotypic regularity of Darwin's irregular phenotypic variations.

In a similar way, at the turn of this century, Freud's theory of the neuroses displaced earlier theories of "satanic possession."[1] Freud also postulated that infantile sexuality and the Oedipal Conflict were universal, and he argued that seemingly irregular, "accidental" slips of the tongue and pen were, in fact, regular in that they were predictable symbols of underlying wishes, motives and desires. In this way, Newton, Darwin, and Freud were all modern in their assumptions regarding the progress, universality and regularity of the natural and social worlds.

The Modern Family

The modern principles of progress, universality, and regularity were believed to apply to the family as well as to society as a whole. Just as society was seen as advancing from a feudal system to democracy, so the family was regarded as evolving from polygamy to monogamy. The modern nuclear family, with one parent working and one parent staying home to rear the children, was taken to be a further evolutionary advance. The theory was that as societies evolved and grew more efficient, social roles became increasingly differentiated and specialized. In the nuclear family, the father as breadwinner and the mother as homemaker were evidence of progressive role differentiation.

The modern nuclear family was also regarded as the family form that would eventually be universal and predominate in modern civilization. Societies in which the nuclear family was not the norm were looked down upon as underdeveloped and

3

primitive. In the same way, the modern nuclear family was also regarded as the most regular kinship arrangement and, by extension, the most moral. Family configurations that deviated from the nuclear norm — whether two-parent-working, single-parent, or adoptive families — were not only regarded as irregular but also as morally inferior. The nuclear family was thus the standard against which all other family forms were evaluated.

Sentiments of the Modern Nuclear Family

Any particular family form can be defined by its unique sentiments, values, and perceptions.[2] As explained in the following pages, the sentiments of the nuclear family reflected the romantic idealism and the commitment to role differentiation that dominated Western societies during the modern era.

A primary sentiment of the modern family was *romantic love* — the belief that there is one and only one person who is put on earth just for us. Once we encounter that person, there is love at first sight. After a brief courtship, we then marry and live happily ever after. It was this sentiment that gave virginity its value in the modern era, when virginity was a commodity reserved for the one person you were destined to mate with. There was a double standard of course, but in theory at least, virginity on the part of the future wife could be exchanged for marital fidelity on the part of the future husband. And for many couples, the romance did last a lifetime, although others were less fortunate. A commitment to romantic love kept some couples (and their children) in relationships that were unhappy at best or abusive at worst.

A second sentiment of the nuclear family was that of *maternal love*. Maternal love was seen as an instinctive need on the part of a mother to build a nest (make a home) and to nurture and rear her children. Inasmuch as the maternal instinct was believed to be universal, women who did not display it — or did not display it to the extent that the community believed it should be displayed — were regarded as unnatural and deviant. Mater-

4

nal love was also believed to be regular in that it remained un-flagging throughout the lifetime of the child. This belief in maternal love worked against the widespread acceptance of early childhood education, as young children were thought to be best cared for by their mothers, inside their own homes.

A third nuclear family sentiment was that of *domesticity*. During the later stages of the modern era, with the spread of in-dustrialization and the movement of workers from farms to the cities and factories, the home became seen a place of peace, quiet and nurturance. Factories were huge, hot, noisy, and clut-tered. Workers on an assembly line were deadened by the rou-tine and often treated as interchangeable bodies by their employers. The home, in contrast, was warm, clean, and com-fortable. There, the father — though treated as a non-entity in the factory — was the recognized master in his own domain. Mothers, meanwhile, were the major purveyors of warmth, nur-turance, and support to all family members.

To be sure, not all men worked in factories, but office work was also usually routine and tedious. The later stages of the modern era gave rise to efficiency experts devoted to making workers another cog in an ever more smooth-running, time-saving machine. In such an environment, when work is sheer drudgery and workers are dehumanized, the home takes on a very special glow and enchantment. Perhaps because parents viewed the home as "A Haven in a Heartless World," they saw it as such for the child, as well.[3] The reluctance to send children to nursery school and even to kindergarten may have reflected — in part, at least — this view of the outside world (including school) as harsh, dreary, and unwelcoming.

Another of the modern family sentiments was the value placed on *togetherness*. In a marriage founded on romantic love, and in a home nurtured by maternal love and domesticity, family relationships became all-important. Meal times, family outings, and activities took precedence over all other professional, so-cial, and recreational opportunities and invitations. This may have led to what was called "Momism" and some over-protectiveness of children, but it also gave children a strong sense of family, as well as the feeling of security that came from knowing that their parents were strongly committed to them.

The perception of parents in the nuclear family was that they were intuitively *knowledgeable* about child-rearing. This perception was grounded in the fact that most young people had grown up in large and extended families, and thus had a lot of experience with children at different age levels while they were growing up. Pediatricians and child psychologists who wrote for parents emphasized the characteristics of children that could be expected at successive age levels, on the assumption that given this information, parents would have a better understanding of the child's behavior and be able to respond in a more sympathetic and appropriate manner.

Overall, the children in the modern nuclear family were perceived as *innocent* and in need of adult protection as well as guidance. The perception of childhood innocence was a natural complement to the sentiments of maternal love and domesticity. The maternal instinct was necessary because young children were innocent and helpless, and therefore required care and nurturance to survive. Domesticity created the needed safe haven in which children could be nourished and socialized. It also resulted in the home being a child-friendly place where children could go into the cupboards and create playthings out of muffin tins and rolling pins.

While this characterization of the nuclear family is correct in broad strokes, it is important to acknowledge the numerous variations of these sentiments and perceptions. In many immigrant families, for example, children often conveyed the culture to their parents, and in some respects, parent and child roles were reversed. In such families, children often spoke English better than their parents and were more fluent readers. In addition, conflicts between the American values and those of the "old country" often led to serious conflicts and rifts between parents and their children. The togetherness of these families was often challenged by the temptations of the larger society, as well.

Likewise, it is also important not to mythologize the nuclear family. Despite the notion of romantic love, many marriages were actually made for practical, family, or economic reasons, and more than a few were less than happy. Spousal and child abuse were certainly present in nuclear families, and so too were infidelity, alcoholism, addictions, and abandonment. While society on the whole was child-friendly, not all nuclear families were, and many of the dysfunctions found in today's families were common in the modern era. They simply were not publicized in the way that they are today.

Modern Childhood

The invention of childhood in the modern era was shaped by Enlightenment-induced changes in society and the family. For example, the modern emphasis upon the advancement of knowledge through observation and experiment led, among other things, to the observation and study of children. It was the "baby biographers" of the seventeenth and eighteenth centuries who helped to focus attention on the unique aspects of childhood and distinguish the early childhood period from the later stages of childhood. These biographies not only noted the play of young children but also the innovative language constructions that are unique to this period. Centuries later, near the end of the modern era, charming illustrations continued to be reported:

"Can't you see, I'm barefoot all over."

"I will get up so early that it will still be late."

"Don't put out the light, I can't see how to sleep."[4]

Back at the start of the twentieth century, child psychologists described another characteristic unique to young children —their difficulty comprehending abstract terms. In 1899, Taylor, for example, gives the following examples of young children's "mishearing" proverbs.

> "A little friend of mine was given the text: 'The Son of man came into the world not to be ministered unto, but to minister.' She went off repeating it to herself and returned a few minutes later saying, 'The Son of man came not to be preachered unto but to preacher.'" Likewise the same child hearing that 'A double-minded man is unstable in all of his ways,' announced that 'A double-minded man is in the stable all the time.'"[5]

During this same era, pioneering early childhood educators and psychologists were making other important observations about the uniqueness of young children. As we shall see in the next chapter, Froebel believed that young children needed to learn the language of forms before learning the language of words.[6] Likewise, Montessori argued that early childhood was a "sensitive period" during which exercise of the senses was crucial.[7] Freud theorized that the early years encompassed the all-important psychosexual oral, anal, and genital stages.[8] Piaget pointed out that early childhood was a period in which children engaged in a great deal of egocentric and magical thinking.[9]

Taken together, these ideas formed the basis of the modern conception of early childhood. It was a period of linguistic creativity but also of linguistic concreteness and an inability to deal with abstractions. It was a sensitive period for the full realization of the senses and for healthy development of the child's psychosexual being. And it was also a period of egocentric and magical thinking. All of these ideas helped to differentiate early childhood from the other stages of the human life cycle.

Even so, the modern idea of childhood incorporated the standard beliefs in progress, universality, and regularity. All children were assumed to progress through the same stages at roughly the same ages. The stages were universal in that there were no exceptions. And finally, the stages were regular, with later stages never appearing before the early stages. Modern childhood was thus different from other psychological stages in structure and content, but it operated according to the same general laws and principles.

Modern Parenting and Early Childhood Education

Comments about modern parenting and early childhood education practices will be made throughout this book, but one critical aspect of them both deserves further consideration here. That has to do with the fact that American parents accepted the modern idea of early childhood as a separate and unique life stage, but they tended to reject the idea of early childhood education. In pre-World War II America, kindergarten education was not mandatory and was offered by fewer than half of our public schools. When it was offered, kindergarten was usually a half-day affair during which children participated in dramatic and block play, listened to stories, and engaged in arts and crafts activities. Froebel's carefully designed sequence of instructional gifts to children (see chapter 2) was rarely followed.

Nursery schools, which appeared in the early 1920s in this country, were also few in number. Such schools were either a luxury for the wealthy, or, under the label of "day care," a place for children of the working poor or indigent. In general, early childhood was seen as a unique period of innocence, during which children were best nurtured by their mothers at home rather than educated at school. Perhaps this is one reason Montessori's program, which she demonstrated with a model class at the 1916 World's Fair in San Francisco, was not well received by America's modern nuclear parents.

The Postmodern World View

The postmodern era has been germinating for a long time. It is probably best perceived not as a revolt against the beliefs of modernity, but rather as a set of attitudes and efforts intended to correct and modify modern ideas that have become outdated or corrupted, or that have proven to be overly broad or narrow. Like the modern era, the postmodern era began as a Western phenomenon. And as with the start of the modern era, the postmodern transformation is not happening all at once, but at different times in different places and in a variety of social institutions.

Like the modern world view, the postmodern world view has its own basic paradigm and correlated themes. The modern perspective tended to reject the past as primitive and to portray non-Western cultures as inferior. In contrast, a postmodern perspective values much of what has been created by earlier generations and appreciates the cultural achievements of contemporary non-Western cultures.

Modern thinkers paid homage to the ideal of freedom for the universal common man, but this was often limited to a male, Anglo-Saxon, Christian common man. A postmodern world view honors human diversity as much as it does our human commonalities.

The modern belief in the unmitigated benefits of scientific and technological development ignored their potential to create ever more powerful weapons of mass destruction, and their contribution to the degradation of the environment. In this and other ways, modern beliefs were not entirely wrong, but they were often overly idealized and blind to the dark side of human nature, scientific discovery, and technological development.

Modern thinkers celebrated reason as the engine of human progress. Today we recognize, however, that rational arguments have also been used to justify inhumane practices such as slavery, colonialism, imperialism, and fascism. Postmodern thinkers venerate language rather than reason as the true rootstock of human existence. This ascendance of language over reason began in the last century, as nineteenth century philosophers such as Nietzsche,[10] Wittgenstein,[11] and the religious philosopher Kierkegaard[12] all played "language games" to demonstrate that there is no such thing as "pure" reason and that our thinking can never be entirely abstracted from our language. Through their use of parody, irony, and satire, these writers demonstrated that language is inherently ambiguous, and that the truths of reason, which employs language, must therefore be ambiguous as well.

When language, rather than reason, is taken as the foundation model for how the world works, an alternative set of themes moves into prominence. Languages do not progress, or at least not necessarily in a positive way. For example, "Franglais" and "TexMex" are language developments that many people do not regard as evidence of linguistic progress. Instead, what characterizes languages are their *differences* from one another and their *embeddedness* within a social, cultural, and historical context. Language is always *particular* to a given culture at a given time, and even within the same country, language varies greatly depending on the community in which it is employed.

Postmodern writers are therefore much more concerned with identifying our social and cultural differences than with demonstrating civilization's unilinear progress. While reason may be taken as universal to mankind, language surely is not. The potential for language is, of course, a human characteristic and is universal in that sense. Yet once this potential is realized , there is no language common to all. Likewise, even though languages can be translated, every language contains idiomatic expressions and cultural meanings that cannot be captured precisely in the words of another language. This leads postmodern writers to focus more on *domain-specific* issues and discourses, rather than on grand universals.

Finally, language — in contrast to reason — is often *irregular* rather than regular. While there are many regular grammatical and spelling rules, there are also many exceptions. English pluralization provides a good example. While *boy* and *girl* are regularly pluralized as *boys* and *girls*, *man* and *woman* are irregularly pluralized as *men* and *women*. Indeed, regularity in

11

language can sometimes be a negative. "Trite" or "hackneyed" phrases and metaphors show how regularity can become "too much of a good thing." Accordingly, many postmodern writers consider the irregular (in science with the chaotic, and in art with post-impressionism) as legitimate and as worthy of exploration as the regular.

These postmodern themes of difference, particularity, and irregularity are increasingly being noted in science, the arts, and industry, as well as other areas of our society. They can also be seen in the transformation of the modern nuclear family into the postmodern "permeable" family.

The Postmodern Permeable Family

Postmodern families have become permeable in that increases in the divorce rate and the number of live-in, unmarried relationships have made leaving existing families and joining new families much easier and more common. This new openness can be seen in the variety of permeable family kinship patterns that now exist in most communities. These patterns include the traditional nuclear family, two-parent-working families, single-parent families, adoptive families, and remarried families.

Generally, the traditional nuclear family, when psychologically healthy and financially secure, may still provide the least stressful pattern of child-rearing — at least for children. Nonetheless, all of the permeable family configurations can provide equally effective support for the successful rearing of children, given the same preconditions.

During the modern era, the traditional nuclear family was regarded as the universal family form towards which all families were evolving. From a postmodern perspective, however, no one permeable family form is necessarily superior to any other. Moreover, there is now a general recognition that the most important determinant of successful child-rearing is the emotional climate of the family (authoritarian, authoritative, neglectful, rejecting), rather than its kinship structure.

Irregular patterns of childrearing, marriage and remarriage are so common that diversity of kinship patterns is now the rule. The permeable family thus echoes the postmodern themes of difference, particularity, and irregularity.

Families have also become permeable to the extent that boundaries between homeplace and workplace and between private and public life have become much more porous and open than they were in the modern era. The increased popularity of home offices, in which communication and computer technologies enable parents to work at home and shift back and forth between the roles of parent and businessperson or professional, are a prime example of this trend.

Sentiments of the Permeable Family

The sentiments of the permeable family also sound postmodern themes. In the permeable family, the sentiment of romantic love has given way to the sentiment of *consensual love*. With the sexual revolution of the 1960s and the social acceptance of premarital sex, virginity — the linchpin of romantic love —lost its value as a medium of exchange. Single men and women now have sexual relations with partners whom they have no intention of marrying, and sexual relations are often entered into by mutual consent and without a lifelong commitment. In fact, young people today marry knowing that divorce is as likely as living together happily ever after.

The sentiment of the modern family, maternal love, has been transformed by the social reality of working mothers. What has replaced it is the new sentiment of *shared parenting*. Rather than the sole responsibility of the mother, today parenting is an occupation that is to be shared with the father, relatives, and nonparental caregivers. It is certainly true, of course, that despite this changed sentiment, mothers still do the "lion's share" of child-rearing and homemaking. Still, fathers do more in the way of childcare and homemaking today than was true in the modern era. Likewise, out-of-home care—while still far less than adequate—is more acceptable and available than it was even a few decades ago. This new sentiment of shared parenting, along with some other key aspects of the postmodern conception of childhood, has helped fuel the extraordinary growth of early childhood education programs.

The modern family sentiment of domesticity has also been unseated, in this case by the postmodern sentiment of *urbanity*. With the advent of television, inexpensive cars, superhighways, jet air travel and more recently the Internet, families have become much more involved with the external world than they were during modern times, when the family was sheltered from the larger society. This can be seen in the way many young children now routinely fly on jet aircraft and dine out at restaurants.

In addition, as noted earlier, service work has replaced factory work, and home offices have become much more commonplace, making the difference between homeplace and workplace much less stark than it was when most work was done in factories. For many people, home is now a place to do work rather than be sheltered from it, so the boundaries between homeplace and workplace — and public and private life — are much more fluid than they were during the modern era.

Another new and important sentiment of the postmodern permeable family is the new value placed on *autonomy*. In effect, each family member's needs and priorities — whether occupational, educational, or recreational — often take precedence over family-oriented activities. In the modern family, where togetherness reigned, having meals together was valued above individual desires and preferences. For permeable family members, however, soccer practice, music lessons, and business meetings are likely to be reasons for missing a meal together. If the nuclear home was a haven, the permeable family home is more like a busy railway station, with people coming in

14

for some brief rest and nurturance before moving out on another track.

The perception of parents in the permeable family is that they need to learn about *techniques* for raising their children. Many of today's parents have grown up in small nuclear families and attended age-graded schools. As a result, they have had little experience with children of different age levels while they were growing up. They often lack the intuitive knowledge of their parents, who grew up in larger and more extended families. Books, articles, and videos now explain specific techniques for handling a wide range of child-raising issues. Yet the focus on technique has sometimes been accompanied by a lack of information about normal patterns of growth and development, leaving parents to find out for themselves which techniques work with children at different age levels. Techniques are most effective when they are developmentally appropriate, and few work well with children at all age levels.

One of the most significant changes in regard to the reinvention of childhood is that the child viewed as innocent in the modern era has been reinvented as *competent* — ready and able to deal with all of life's vicissitudes in the postmodern era. This perception of child competence did not grow out of any new theories or research findings; rather, it developed because postmodern families need competent children. We need children who can adapt to out-of-home care at an early age, who can cope with divorce and single parenting, and who will not be unduly upset by the graphic violence and lurid sexuality so prominent on our television screens. We need children who identify and evade strangers, and who know the difference between good and bad touches. For reasons such as these, the new perception of childhood competence was invented to meet the needs of adults and our society as a whole.

In describing the postmodern permeable family, I have presented an ideal type that cannot match every real family in every respect. Today, in fact, most families probably combine nuclear and permeable family sentiments, values and perceptions. Many postmodern mothers, for example, combine the sentiments of maternal love with shared parenting, and so take major responsibility for their children's care while entrusting some of it to others. Likewise, many families, though urbane in some respects, manage to maintain certain family rituals that support a feeling of togetherness. And while technique is certainly emphasized today, publications such as *Parents* magazine and authors such as T. Berry Brazelton[13] and Penelope Leach[14] emphasize development as much as technique. This blending of the modern and the postmodern is itself an example of the postmodern *pastiche*, in which elements from various sources or eras are combined.

The Postmodern Concept of Early Childhood

The contemporary reinvention of early childhood is in keeping with the postmodern ideas that have transformed society and the family. A postmodern perspective on early childhood emphasizes its differences, particularity, and irregularity, rather than seeing it as progressive, universal, and regular.

This perspective acknowledges that young children do not all grow at the same rate and in the same manner, as the concept of regularity would have it. Nor are the characteristics of young children as universal as was once believed. For example, though early childhood may be a time for developing the senses, some children may develop one or another sense to a greater extent than the others. Likewise, although growth is regular for most children, some bright children may skip stages and other children may take different paths to attain the same skill. At the end of his career, Jean Piaget discovered that some children may attain "conservation," the understanding that a quantity remains the same in amount despite a change in appearance, through a different avenue than the one he had previously supposed was the only path.

So, the postmodern reinvention of early childhood is not so much a reinvention of the content and structure of young children's thought and language, so much as it is a reinvention of the rules and principles that govern the acquisition and use of that content and structure. This new perspective focuses on the unique characteristics and circumstances of individual children, including the societal and familial changes discussed earlier in this chapter.

Postmodern Child-rearing and Early Childhood Education

Inasmuch as postmodern childrearing and education are discussed throughout this book, only some general comments seem needed here. Perhaps the most striking change in the way young children are cared for is that the changes in society and in the family have finally led to widespread acceptance of the value of early childhood education, the modern idea advocated by Froebel and Montessori. Early childhood programs have proliferated across the country as a result.

In addition, and as part of the postmodern reinvention of childhood, parents and educators are acknowledging young children differently than was true in the past. Parents are more aware of and accepting of individual differences, and many early childhood programs now provide for the "inclusion" of special needs children and incorporate multi-cultural curricula. In this way, the postmodern reinvention of childhood is making life easier for many of today's young children, at the same time that many other changes in the family and our society may be making life more difficult for them.

Conclusion

The postmodern reinvention of childhood is both part of and the result of the profound changes that are reshaping our families and society. These changes pose daunting challenges to today's parents and teachers, and require new parenting and educational practices that can both modify these changes and help young children adapt to them. In attempting to develop these practices, we first need to consider the theories and practices developed during the modern era, to see which aspects remain valid in the postmodern era and which now need to be reinvented.

Chapter 2

Modern Inventors of Childhood

Our understanding of young children and how they should be reared and educated was shaped by a number of outstanding modern thinkers. The most important innovators in the field of early childhood education— Freidrich Froebel, Maria Montessori, and Rudolph Steiner — introduced original ideas that continue to be the foundation for much of contemporary early childhood education. In the field of psychology, too, the emphasis has been on the early years of life. Psychoanalyst Sigmund Freud emphasized the importance of the early years for later personality development, and his views had an enormous influence on the ways young children have been raised and taught. Three of the more recent "grandmasters" — Jean Piaget, Lev Vygotsky, and Erik Erikson — did not limit themselves to this age period, but, nonetheless, their work has probably had its greatest impact on early childhood education.

All these grandmasters of education and psychology held to the fundamental tenets of modernity — progress, universality, and regularity. For example, they all assumed there was a universal "child nature" that remained the same in different times and different places. This belief led these modern inventors to formulate what might be called "grand" theories of child pedagogy and development, which were offered as valid accounts of children's development regardless of the historical period or the particular society in which the child lived. To the extent that these models were linked to the physical characteristics of our species (e.g. sensory abilities or brain development), they still have a legitimate claim to universality. However, as we shall see, facets of each theory now appear untenable from a postmodern perspective, while other aspects remain valid.

Freidrich Froebel (1782-1852)

Freidrich Froebel was the first to emphasize the educational importance of the early years of life, and he can truly be called the "father of early childhood education." Although trained as a crystallographer, he left his chosen discipline to become a teacher. To this end he studied with Pestalozzi — the first educator to translate Rousseau's radical educational philosophy into practice. From Pestalozzi and Rousseau, Froebel acquired a distrust of formal education and a faith in children's ability to learn from their own self-initiated and self-directed activity. But he was unique in believing that young children can and should be educated before they enter school.

The name for the early educational program he invented, "kindergarten" (children's garden), came to him during a walk in the woods. In his school, Froebel offered no formal instruction in morals and character, because he thought these qualities were naturally acquired as children learned to care for living things. Plants and animals therefore became a fixture of most kindergartens.

Also at the heart of Froebel's kindergarten philosophy was a conviction that young children learn through play. To encourage this, he created songs and games for mothers to use with their infants. Traditional games like "This Little Piggy" and songs like "Happy Birthday" can be traced back to Froebel.

Perhaps Froebel's most important contributions to early childhood education were what he called his "gifts" (the materials used in kindergarten) and "occupations" (the ways the materials could be used).[1] There were twenty gifts, ranging from simple forms (sphere, square, and cylinder) to entire sets of wooden geometric shapes in many different sizes and colors.

There were also colored paper geometric figures that had adhesive backs, so that they could be pasted together into different shapes. One gift included a wooden pin with which children could create patterns by punching small holes in sheets of paper. Another gift was a set of sticks and dried peas that could be put together into various shapes (the forerunner of today's Tinker Toys™).

What Froebel hoped to achieve with these gifts and occupations, and with the kindergarten experience as a whole, is aptly summarized by Brosterman:

> "The end result of this all-encompassing instruction was the creation of a sensitive, inquisitive child with an uninhibited curiosity and genuine respect for nature, family and society."[2]

Put another way, Froebel believed that early childhood education should provide children with a positive orientation towards life and learning, not just a collection of facts and skills.

The concept of kindergarten caught on quickly in many parts of the world, and by the end of the nineteenth century thousands of kindergartens were part of the educational landscape. Unfortunately, because Froebel did not maintain control over either his materials or teacher training, many of the gifts were disregarded and kindergartens became a place for play, socialization, and exercise, rather than for education as Froebel had envisioned it. The play-oriented kindergarten was in keeping with the modern nuclear family's emphasis on childhood innocence and maternal love.

It was not until the postmodern period and the accompanying reinvention of childhood that Froebel's belief in the educational importance of the early years became more accepted in this country. But Froebel, like Montessori after him, understood education as deriving from the child's own activity, not from books and lessons.

Maria Montessori (1870-1952)

Maria Montessori was the first female physician in Italy, and after her graduation she worked first with retarded and then with low-income children. Challenged to tame young children in high-rise apartments, where they were regarded as noisy and destructive by the owners, she ended up creating an early childhood education program that soon became world famous.

Based on her careful observations of young children, Montessori developed an innovative set of learning tools from materials originally devised for use with older retarded learners. Montessori recognized that young children, like those with limited intelligence, can successfully engage in many activities once thought to be too complex or difficult for them. Their success simply requires that the tasks be made compatible with their level of competence.

Montessori looked at the world from the young child's point of view and appreciated that at least some limitations were the result of living in a world tailored to adult size and strength. It was Montessori, for example, who introduced child-sized chairs, tables, plates, silver, cups, and glasses specially fabricated for her classrooms. These and many other of Montessori's contributions to the early childhood classroom have become so commonplace that we no longer recognize them as her inventions.

In order to help young children realize their abilities to the full, Montessori based her approach on the insight that preschool children are most given to learning through their senses:

> "Now the period of life between the ages of three and seven years covers a period of rapid physical development. It is the time for the formation of the sense activities as related to the intellect...This is, therefore, the time when we should methodically direct the sense stimuli, in such a way that the sensations which he receives shall develop in a

rational way. This sense training will prepare the ordered foundation upon which he may build up a clear and strong mentality."[3]

Montessori introduced many different materials for helping young children develop their sensorial abilities and their motor skills. Among the learning tools she employed were wool skeins of different colors to help children distinguish subtle differences in hue, as well as bells of different sizes to facilitate children's pitch recognition. Montessori also believed that children should learn to write before they learn to read. To further this activity, she devised a set of large, sandpaper-covered wooden letters that the children could identify by touch as well as by sight, and which they could combine to make words. These and other learning tools created by Montessori became the basis for a goodly number of what today are called "educational" toys. The form-board picture puzzles so commonplace today are, to illustrate, fashioned after those first used in the Montessori classroom.

Many of Montessori's materials were self-teaching in the sense that children themselves could discover when they were going amiss. With the form-board picture puzzles, for example, children can easily recognize when a piece they are trying to insert does or does not fit properly. In the same way, children can themselves appreciate when objects that vary in size are not correctly ordered. Montessori believed that young children have a natural desire for regularity, and if given the materials and the opportunity, they will arrange materials symmetrically. Likewise, if children learn that everything has its own place, as it does in a Montessori classroom, children will also want to put materials where they belong after they have been used.

Montessori felt that young children are best educated in an environment (she called it a "prepared environment") rich in manipulative sensory materials, which children can move on their own and learn from through their own activities. Montessori was convinced that learning in such an environment fostered young children's intellectual growth and their independence as individuals, because at this stage children have a good sense of what they want to and need to learn. That is why children in early childhood education programs can do with much less adult direction in regard to the curriculum than is needed at later age levels.

Montessori was also convinced that the education of the senses in young children should precede any attempts to teach them symbols. (Froebel had also argued that children should learn the language of forms before they learn the language of words.) In the early years, the names may be more confusing than helpful, as children can distinguish the several geometric forms, the hues of the rainbow, and variations in size without having names for these differences. Once children have the discriminations well in hand, however, the names and labels are easily attached and have a significance they would not have had were they presented before the discriminations were clearly established. Here Montessori's views go against our intuitive adult inclination to use the label as an aid to teaching a discrimination, rather than using it as the mark of its achievement.

Despite her brilliant insights, Montessori remained a woman of her times in certain respects. For example, she seemed to have accepted the Puritanical notion of children's waywardness, at least to the extent that imagination and play were a waste of time, even if not the Devil's work. Her dictum that "play is the child's work" ignores the fact that play is *assimilative* — a transformation of the world in the service of the self — while work is *accommodative* — a transformation of the self in service of the world.[4] This view led Montessori to write that if a child could imagine fairies and ogres, why couldn't he or she imagine cities in America, such as New York. In this and other ways Montessori believed that imagination should be put to practical, not "idle," purposes.

Sigmund Freud (1856-1939)

In his writings, Freud described the infancy and early childhood stages of sexual development as critically linked to personality development.[5] However, Freud used sex in the broad sense of a pattern of excitation that built up gradually and was abruptly relieved. This pattern is common to our appetitive and eliminatory functions, as well as to our sexual ones. To illustrate, our desire for food increases gradually and is diminished rather quickly after we ingest food. Our sexual organs operate in the same way, with sexual excitement building gradually to a peak and then becoming abruptly reduced after climax. In these patterns, the sudden release of tension is experienced as pleasurable, and due to this pattern of excitation Freud contended that the mouth and the anus could be considered sexual.

Freud also posited the notion of critical periods somewhat like the ones proposed by Montessori. Freud, however, related these stages to later pathology as well as to initial development. He argued that the pleasure-giving-instinct was centered in the oral region during infancy, but shifted to the anal region during the second year of life and then moved to the genital zone by age four or five. All of these zones continue to provide tension and pleasure throughout childhood and the rest of life, but there is a critical time for the healthy patterning of their arousal and satisfaction.

Consider the oral stage that occurs during the first year of life. If the infant's hunger needs are met when they arise, and if the infant is neither over nor underfed, he or she will develop healthy attitudes towards food and eating, enjoying food for its own sake and not as a substitute for other types of satisfaction. On the other hand, if an infant's appetitive needs are not met when he or she is hungry or thirsty, or if the child is underfed or overfed, the infant may become *fixated* at this level. As a consequence, as the child matures, he or she will continue to seek satisfaction mainly through oral activities. Orally fixated children

25

may continue to suck their thumbs and overeat as a means of reducing stress.

At the next stage, which occurs during the second year of life, similar outcomes are possible. If the child is bowel- and bladder-trained without pressure, and with thoughtfulness and sensitivity, he or she will move through this period without attaching undue importance to these activities. On the other hand, if parents are overly demanding about bowel and bladder control, or if they allow the child to wet and soil well beyond the age when this is developmentally appropriate, the child may get fixated at the anal level and have an unusual need for order and routine. Such children have the most trouble sharing their toys with other children, and when anxious, anally fixated children will engage in repetitive activities such as kicking or banging something.

Towards the age of four or five, the sexual instinct moves to the genital area. At this stage, however, the sexual instinct takes a new turn. The oral and anal drives are *autoerotic* in the sense that they can be satisfied by the child's own actions. While the sexual drive can also be relieved in this way, it can also be satisfied — and more completely so — through sexual intercourse with another person. At the genital stage, therefore, the sexual instinct is no longer simply sensorial, but becomes cognitive and social as well. During this period, we see the first instance of what Freud called the "family romance," (more technically, the Oedipus complex) as the child becomes romantically attached to the parent of the opposite sex. Without understanding how the parent can do this (the young child, of course, has no knowledge of sexual intimacy), the child nonetheless looks to the father or mother as someone who can satisfy the genital yearning.

The family romance, however, presents the young child with a problem in that it puts the child in competition with the parent of the same sex for the love of the opposite-sex parent. In fantasy, the child may actually imagine getting rid of his or her rival. This helps to explain why young girls may become seductive with their fathers, while young boys may try to display their physical prowess to their mothers. If parents accept this behavior as charming and amusing but do not get caught up in it, the child will eventually resolve the conflict by identifying with the parent of the same sex. It is in this way that the child acquires a sense of gender identity. Such identification also wins the parent of the opposite sex vicariously and resolves the need to get rid of the opposite-sex parent.

On the other hand, if something interferes with this process, the child may experience difficulties in relating to peers and other adults. Should the parents tease or shame the young child's efforts at seduction, for example, the child may become fearful of taking the initiative in social situations. He or she, for example, might want to play with other children but be afraid to volunteer for fear of being repulsed and rejected. Other children who have been overly encouraged in their seductiveness may become inappropriately sexually aggressive towards their peers.

As children move into childhood proper, about the age of six or seven, they enter what Freud called the *latency* stage. During this period, the sexual instincts become subordinated to the ego instincts — those concerned with adaptation to the physical and social world. Like Montessori, therefore, Freud saw childhood proper as a period dedicated to acquiring the basic "tool skills" (reading, writing, and arithmetic), knowledge, and values for living successfully within society. Children who have not successfully negotiated the earlier stages may encounter some difficulty during this period. For example, a child who has not successfully resolved the family romance and acquired a gender identity may extend his or her conflicts into the classroom. A boy with an unresolved Oedipus complex may see a female teacher as someone to be won over by shows of bravado. A girl may have difficulty dealing with a female teacher whom she perceives as a rival.

27

Also like Montessori, Freud was a modern writer who took the modern nuclear family and the modern conception of early childhood for granted. In our postmodern world, however, with the permeable family the predominant family form and a reinvented early childhood, some aspects of Freud's theory seem dated. How is it possible, for example, for children growing up in a single-parent family to develop an Oedipus complex? Likewise, Freud saw the emotional problems of children as stemming from one or another form of sexual fixation, frustration, repression or abuse. Today, we recognize that many children's emotional problems originate in the overwhelming stress (inordinate demands for adaptation) the child is experiencing, rather than from sexually related trauma.

Rudolph Steiner (1861-1925)

Rudolph Steiner was a German philosopher and educator whose pedagogical ideas are now translated into practice in the Waldorf Schools.[6] Steiner was deeply concerned that the growth of modern technology was moving education away from many of our most fundamental human qualities — our feelings, our emotions, our bodily rhythms, and our need to express these. He believed that education was increasingly emphasizing the intellectual and the technical to the neglect of these other all-important components of our humanity. To counter these tendencies, Steiner devised an educational system that he believed addressed all facets of the human personality in their complex interactions.

While Steiner took a developmental approach to education, which he saw as being comprised of three stages, he derived his pedagogy from his observations and from his unique empathy for children, rather than from scientific research. In this respect, he was very much like Montessori.

For Steiner, early childhood is a period when the child's *will* is most in evidence, as young children begin to discover themselves, and to separate themselves from others and from the domination of their parents. In so doing, they often demonstrate a characteristic "willfulness" that is neither bad nor wrong but merely characteristic of this stage. Rather than try to destroy or "break" this willfulness, Steiner suggested that it be recognized and used for educational purposes.

For example, the willfulness of young children also gives them great powers of concentration. They engage in activities with their whole bodies, hearts, and minds, and rarely think about something else when engaged in a particular enterprise. This total concentration is sometimes misread by adults. Young children want to engage themselves totally, and that is why "Do Not Touch!" is so antithetical to them. They want to experience their world totally, by seeing, tasting, hearing, smelling, and touching, as well as holding and rubbing. Steiner therefore concluded that education should provide materials that make such engagement meaningful and productive.

Steiner tied his stages to the child's physical development and placed great emphasis on the child's acquisition of permanent teeth at about the age of six or seven. He argued that with this attainment, the focus of the child's functioning shifts from the realm of will to that of *feeling*, with the child now wanting to engage the world emotionally, not just sensorially. To be sure, the younger child is not devoid of feelings, but these do not dominate his or her orientation. For example, a young child will be happy with a story that entails little more than a series of successive actions, such as *Chicken Little*. In contrast, the older child wants to know how the animals feel — what their fears are, as well as their joys. Along with this orientation to feelings, Steiner also believed that the eruption of the permanent teeth was the indication that a child was ready for formal instruction in reading and math.

Steiner's next stage comes to fruition about seven years after the appearance of the permanent teeth and is coincident with the attainment of puberty. Steiner felt this period was dominated by the third of his basic trilogy of personality components — *mind*. According to Steiner, it is during adolescence that the young person tries to comprehend the world intellectually and conceptually rather than sensorially or emotionally. Will and feeling are not absent, but arise in new and more complex forms that the young person must try to encompass within the sphere of intellect. This is usually not accomplished successfully until the following developmental epoch begins at age twenty-one.

In his pedagogy, Steiner advocated practices that speak to the child's developing physical and spiritual self, as well as to the mind. For example, Steiner advocated that children stay with the same teacher for a number of years, so that teacher and pupils could really get to know and appreciate one another as individuals. Steiner was also a fervent supporter of the arts, believing that they should be a fundamental part of the educational experience, and he suggested that this integration could be accomplished in many different ways. He felt that children should be encouraged to research, write and illustrate their own textbooks, and that when learning about a particular historical period, the children might practice the handicrafts (such as weaving and pottery-making) engaged in by people living in that era.

In many respects, Steiner was one of the most postmodern thinkers to be considered in this chapter. His insistence upon children creating their own curriculum materials preceded the postmodern concept that learning is a constructive, creative activity. Likewise, his insistence on teaching all subjects through the arts ties in with the postmodern emphasis on an integrated curriculum. And Steiner's advocacy of the teacher staying with the same group of children for a number of years is very similar to the postmodern rationale for multi-age grouping. Finally, his insistence upon the importance of narrative, stories, biographies, and historical anecdotes in children's learning is also very postmodern.

Still, Steiner was a product of the modern world and shared the modern conception of early childhood. He assumed that the children he was educating came from two-parent families; shared the same customs, values, and language; and were well fed and well clothed. In this and other ways, his theory tends to assume a universal sociological and psychological child nature. Nonetheless, the Waldorf philosophy that children should be respected as full and independent human beings is totally in keeping with the postmodern notion of particularity, and Waldorf education is exceedingly adaptable to the diversity of children of the postmodern world.

Jean Piaget (1896-1980)

Over the course of his long and productive career, famed Swiss psychologist Jean Piaget talked about early childhood in several different ways. During the first period of his career, when he was employing a sociological model, he wrote of the young child's language and thinking as being largely *egocentric*.[7] In using this term, Piaget did not intend anything pejorative, but rather meant to distinguish the young child's language from the more mature sociocentric discourse and thinking of older children and adults. Young children were egocentric not because they were selfish, but because they were unable to put themselves in another person's position and see things from that point of view.

Piaget used egocentrism to explain several facets of young children's language and thinking. Young children, for example, often speak *at* rather than *to* another person, in the sense that they do not accommodate their responses to what the other person is saying. Piaget called conversations between two preschool children, who seem to be talking to one another but are effectively carrying on separate monologues, *parallel* speech. He also identified egocentrism in children's thinking. A young child, to illustrate, may not be able to correctly identify the right and left hands of someone who is standing opposite him or her — even when the youngster can correctly identify his or her own. Again, this gives evidence of the young child's difficulty in taking a perspective other than his or her own.

Later in his career Piaget adopted a logical model of children's language and thought.[8] Starting from a number of investigations exploring children's ability to "conserve" — to recognize that a quantity remains the same despite a change in its appearance —Piaget introduced the concept of *concrete operations*. These operations usually came into evidence at around the age of six or seven and resembled, in their functioning, the elementary operations of arithmetic. Among other achievements, the attainment of concrete operations made possible the understanding of rules, units and syllogistic reasoning.

It was because young children were not yet capable of these concrete operations that Piaget described their thinking as *pre-operational*. He and his colleagues took great pains to point out, however, that young children still had many powerful mental skills and abilities.[9] Young children, to illustrate, can order objects according to size and classify them as to their common properties. They can also define objects in terms of the actions to be performed on them, realizing that an apple is "to eat" and a car is "to drive." Moreover, pre-operational children can reason, but only *transductively* — from event to event or from fact to fact. A child who asks, "If I eat spaghetti, will I be Italian?" is wondering whether there is a causal connection between two factual circumstances.

It is only when children reach the concrete operations stage that they can fully profit from formal instruction. This is true because only with concrete operations are children capable of reasoning and following rules on which formal instruction (of phonics or multiplication, for example) is based. Attempting to teach children rule- and reason-oriented skills before they have attained concrete operations may be so frustrating that it causes the children to feel they are failures — as one child put it, "a flop in life."

Piaget's discoveries regarding the language and thought of young and school-age children also have other important implications for child-rearing and education. One of the most important is the understanding that children's thinking is different than our own and should therefore not be considered intrinsically bad or wrong. When a young child talks or behaves egocentrically, he or she is acting appropriately for his or her age. Likewise, when a school-age child assumes that a rule is inviolate, we must recognize that this is characteristic of the age group. Learning about the exceptions to rules and that rules are man-made comes later in childhood.

With respect to education, Piaget argued strongly that children move on to concrete operations as a consequence of maturation and of the experiences created by their own actions. It is through the active manipulation of objects in the environment that the child comes to discover their multi-faceted character. (In this respect he echoed Montessori and Steiner in their emphasis upon the importance of manipulative experience for young children.) For Piaget, it was each child's spontaneous activities that were most instrumental in moving him or her towards concrete operations, as in Piaget's example of a young boy who is playing with ten pebbles. The child arranges them in a square, in a circle, and then in a triangle. Suddenly, he comes to the recognition that no matter how he arranges them, the number remains the same. This discovery thus comes about from his own activity upon things, rather than from adult instruction. It is this auto-didactic learning, emphasized by Montessori as well, that is so important for cognitive development.

At the school-age level, Piaget recognized that the teacher must play a more directive role. Children do need help and guidance in learning basic math facts and reading skills. Yet even at the grade school level, children can be given more opportunities to make choices and learn on their own than they are often allowed in the elementary classroom. However, large classes, rigid curricular guidelines, and frequent testing all militate against the kind of choices that would help children take more control over their learning and have a greater sense of ownership of it.

Like Steiner, Piaget was postmodern in many respects. His view of the child constructing reality out of his or her experiences with the environment is a widely accepted tenet of postmodern education. Although he is not often credited for it, Piaget also emphasized the domain-specific nature of learning. That is why he carried out so many investigations of different topics. He recognized that every cognitive content could generate a different type of resistance to acquisition and had to be conceptualized in its own way.

Yet Piaget could not entirely escape the modern conception of early childhood. For example, early in his career he hypothesized that learning to take the other person's point of view was an important prerequisite to further social and cognitive development. In this respect, as in writings about adolescence, Piaget and his colleagues accepted the modern idea that socialization was primarily a matter of perspective-taking and acquiring social roles that were both universal and regular. Indeed, sociologists regarded the evolution of society as involving progressive role differentiation and specialization of function that were assumed to make society more adaptive and efficient. As we shall see in chapter 4, however, the taking of social roles and perspectives are now seen as a matter of acquiring "frames and scripts."

Lev Vygotsky (1896-1934)

Although the Russian psychologist Lev Vygotsky died before the onset of World War II, his work is only now becoming widely known in the West.[10] During his all-too-brief professional life (he died at age 38 from tuberculosis), Vygotsky made important contributions in a number of different areas of psychology. In this country, he is perhaps best known for his theories of language and cognitive development and for his emphasis upon the importance of society and culture in the determination of mental growth.

One of Vygotsky's major contributions was his emphasis upon the importance of *mediation* in the learning and development of young children. Unlike Froebel, Montessori, Steiner, and Piaget, Vygotsky argued that learning is not self-initiated and directed, but rather socially motivated and guided — and so mediated. This mediation is accomplished by the use of mental tools, the foremost of which is language. It is also mediated by adults —parents and teachers — who model problem solving and tool use.

As children develop, we can observe their growing use of language and other mental tools as mediators for adapting to their social world. Young children progressively master language as a means of expressing their needs and as a way of monitoring and guiding their own actions. A young child engaged in an activity can be heard to say, "This goes here," which shows that the child is using language to mediate the action. Young children also learn to use adults as models for the acquisition of various skills, as when infants are first fed by an adult but eventually, by modeling adult action, learn to use a spoon successfully and then to hold a fork so as to maximize its function.

Vygotsky's theories regarding the origins of language and thought are probably his most controversial. He argued that the two are initially separate, and that there is pre-linguistic thought just as there is pre-intellectual language.[11] That is to say, the young infant constructs a conception of the parent long before he or she has a language symbol for that construction. In the same way, a child can use simple words without having any idea as to their meaning. In early childhood, language and thought become increasingly interrelated and interdependent, and only in later childhood do they once again separate.

For Vygotsky, both thought and language are social in origin, and the child learns both by modeling the language and actions of adults in his or her environment. It is for this reason that in early childhood, thought and language are inseparable. As children become more proficient with language, it becomes increasingly internalized, with whispering serving as a step along the way. Eventually, language attains the level of inner speech, which Vygotsky described as "egocentric," as opposed to logical thought, which is social. For Vygotsky, therefore, egocentric speech is the end-product of internalized social speech, whereas for Piaget egocentric speech is a form of individual speech that is eventually given up in favor of social speech.

Another important concept introduced by Vygotsky was that of the *zone of proximal development.* In Vygotsky's view, children do not spontaneously maximize their intellectual abilities when they are left on their own to manipulate their world. Rather, it is adult intervention that enables children to realize their abilities to the full. Suppose, for example, that when an infant is learning to use a spoon, the parent picks up his or her own spoon and begins to eat. Vygotsky believed that an infant who observes this repeated action on the part of the parent will learn to use the spoon correctly more quickly than if the child were to learn it on his or her own. The difference between the time it takes children to attain a skill on their own, and the time it takes to acquire the skill with adult modeling or other intervention, is the zone of proximal development.

It is important to emphasize that Vygotsky, no less than Piaget, understood there were limits to what could be accomplished by adult example. He did not believe that human development itself — as opposed to specific activities — could be *accelerated* by adult modeling. Nonetheless, in his emphasis on the social, Vygotsky provides a useful counterbalance to Piaget's somewhat overly maturational perspective. Piaget often wrote as if children had a developmentally determined need to fully realize their abilities and sought out the stimuli needed for this purpose. Vygotsky, in contrast, focused on the important role adults can play in helping children maximize their developing abilities. Obviously, maturation and experience are both important.

Vygotsky's theories add an important new dimension to the viewpoints that we have already discussed. More than any other writer, Vygotsky emphasized the important role that society plays in shaping children's language and thought. Even so, because he also stated that there are universal phases in the evolution of thought and language which transcend any particular society, he agreed that there are some facets of development that are common to all children, at least in early childhood.

From a practical standpoint, Vygotsky's emphasis on the importance of adult example and modeling applies not just to the domain of manners and morals, but also to learning tool skills and intellectual concepts.[12] It affirms that we, as parents and teachers, play an important role in helping children acquire many different cognitive and social skills. The importance of this kind of learning — or the lack of it — has been shown in research studies documenting that children who have attended an early education center have significantly more literacy and numeracy skills than those who have not.[13]

Like the other writers we have reviewed, Vygotsky was modern in some respects and postmodern in others. In his emphasis upon the importance of language and of society in the child's intellectual growth and development, Vygotsky is quite postmodern. At the same time, however, he elevated the importance of the social to the level of the biological. Living in a Marxist society, Vygotsky's insistence on the universal importance of society is understandable, but it may extend the role of society too far.

Erik Erikson (1902-1994)

A famed psychoanalyst and Pulitzer Prize-winning author, the late Erik H. Erikson was, as a young man, very much influenced by Montessori's ideas. In fact, he was trained as a Montessori teacher, and it was while working in one of the first psychoanalytically oriented nursery schools in Vienna that he became attracted to what became his chosen profession, child psychiatry. After moving to the United States just prior to World War II, Erikson held positions at a number of major universities and became friendly with colleagues teaching sociology and anthropology. With their help, he studied several Indian tribes in the Pacific Southwest. He also worked with war veterans in psychiatric hospitals. Building upon these field and clinical experiences — and upon his therapeutic work with children in private practice — he developed and published a theory of human development that encompassed the whole life cycle.[14] He then continued to elaborate on these views during the remainder of his long and productive career.

Erikson posited that we come into the world with eight bipolar potentialities or social senses that, while present from birth, have a specific period in life that is critical for their full realization. The balance struck between these poles during the critical period is lasting and can only be undone by extraordinary experiences at a later stage. Like Montessori, Erikson believed that the early years were a particularly important period not only for children's intellectual development, but also for their emotional and social development as well. Indeed, four of Erikson's eight stages of human life cycle occur during the first twelve years of life.

With respect to early childhood, Erikson regarded the ages of two to three as a period in which the balance between *autonomy* and *shame* are established, with toilet training serving as a central motor skill for this determination. If parents are relaxed about the achievement, wait for the child's muscles to be sufficiently mature before they introduce training, and do not get angry if the child has an accident, the toddler will develop a sense of autonomy that outweighs any feelings of shame, guilt, or doubt. Such a child will then be willing to take responsibility for his or her own actions and opinions.

While a small amount of shame and doubt can be healthy in preventing an excessive sense of autonomy, too much shame and doubt can be debilitating. Some parents are impatient for the child to be trained well before the child's physical apparatus is sufficiently developed to make this possible. They are very critical and make derogatory remarks about the child's accidents. Growing up under these circumstances, the child may develop a sense of shame and doubt that far outweighs his or her sense of autonomy. Such a child may become, as an adult, reluctant to take responsibility for his or her own actions, and remain insecure and uncertain about his or her own beliefs.

Around the age of four or five, the social polarity between *initiative* and *guilt* has its critical period. Young children at this age have a boundless curiosity and are eager to explore all facets of their world. This is the age of the infamous "why" questions, and it's a period during which children want to take things apart to see how they are made and how they work. If parents are patient and accepting of these explorations, the child will develop a healthy sense of initiative that will outweigh the sense of guilt. As with shame and doubt, a certain amount of guilt is healthy, however, and sometimes children's explorations have to be brought to a halt. If a child attempts to use something that is beyond his or her physical dexterity or unsafe, like a power tool, this cannot be permitted. The child needn't be punished or chastised, but merely informed that the tool is dangerous and that he or she can use it at a later age. In the meantime, a hand-powered screw driver or drill will do.

If, however, parents and care-givers are impatient with the child's efforts at exploration, and if his or her questions are ignored or answered without much thought, the child's sense of initiative may become overburdened by a sense of guilt over having made the exploration or asked the question. Children who leave this stage with a sense of guilt that is much stronger than their sense of initiative may be afraid to undertake tasks on their own, or, having undertaken them, may be reluctant to bring them to completion. This unhealthy balance can be redressed later in life, but it will take a great deal more support and encouragement than would have been necessary to accomplish the same result in early childhood.

As children move into childhood proper, another social polarity becomes the central issue of socialization. At this stage, roughly the ages from 6-12, children deal with the issue of *industry* vs. *inferiority*. This is the time period when young people learn the basic tool skills of reading, writing, and arithmetic, as well as basic concepts of science, history, and literature. If children are encouraged and supported in their efforts to master these skills and knowledge, they attain a sense of industry that far outweighs their sense of inferiority.

In contrast, if the child meets constant failure and adult derision in his or her efforts to learn, then there is a strong likelihood that the child will develop a sense of inferiority that is more powerful than the sense of industry. Again, this unhealthy imbalance can be undone later, but only at a much greater cost in time and effort.

In many ways, Erikson is among the most postmodern of the writers considered in this chapter. He broke with Freud's sexual theories of neurotic behavior and recognized the role of social factors in the determination of emotional distress. He also recognized that emotional problems can originate in adulthood as well as in childhood. Nonetheless, just because his stages are social, they are not likely to be universal. For example, in some societies where women are conditioned to be subservient, shame and doubt may be more adaptive responses for young girls than autonomy, which could lead to punishment.

Conclusion

We have now reviewed how different modern theorists conceptualized and articulated the modern conception of early childhood. All agree that the experiences encountered during the early years of life are critical for later development of the individual. Nonetheless, the grandmasters fall into two distinct camps with regard to child nature. Froebel, Montessori, Steiner, and Piaget reflect the Rousseauian idea that the child is essentially good and that society corrupts the child through its child-rearing and educational practices. In contrast, Freud, Vygotsky, and Erikson argue that the child's primary need is to be socialized by adults.

Despite their differences, these writers were all modern in their focus upon the ways in which young children differ from older children, and their relative neglect of the enormous diversity *among* young children of the same age. So, while many of their insights about young children's cognitive, social, and emotional development remain valid today, these insights now have to be integrated into a reinvention of childhood that takes into account individual, social, ethnic, and racial differences within the same age level.

Chapter 3

Reinventing
Language Development

During the modern era, the language of young children was one of the characteristics most often used to distinguish these children from older children and adults. As noted earlier, young children's novel language creations and their misunderstanding of abstract terms were used as hallmarks of this developmental period. And in keeping with the principles of modernity, language development was portrayed as progressive, universal, and regular.

Now that we have moved into the postmodern era, this modern conception of children's language must be reconstructed to incorporate our broader and deeper understanding of the complexity of language. Particularly in this country, where the influences of so many different languages and cultures continue to be felt, it's easy to see how and why modern progressive, universal, and regular portrayal of young children's language has given way to a postmodern appreciation of language difference, particularity and irregularity. The controversies over "Black English" and bilingual education, as well as the decades-long debate about the "best" way to teach reading, are just a few examples of the trends that have led to a postmodern reinvention of language development.

It must be said that a straightforward, descriptive approach to the maturation of children's language — tracing the progressive appearance of nouns, verbs, sentence structure, etc. — is not wrong but is extremely limited. Moreover, today we also appreciate that young children's language development also plays a crucial role in their intellectual and social/emotional development, as well as their sense of identity and self-esteem.

In fact, the field of early language development has itself become so extensive that only a few, key illustrations of the postmodern reinvention of language development can be presented here, starting with a brief historical overview.

Language Development: From Modern to Postmodern

Psychologists of the modern era were most concerned with children's vocabulary growth, sentence production, and verbal comprehension. By 1900, there was general agreement that young children learn the names of objects and qualities before they learn the terms for relations and conjunctions, and that they speak simple sentences before they utilize more complex constructions. Psychologists also agreed that young children have difficulty with abstractions.

Early psychologists were also concerned with the origins and history of language because of the belief in the *recapitulation theory*, the idea that the child repeats in his or her development the history of the language development of the species. Psychologists compared, for example, the phonetics of "primitive" languages and those of young children, finding that children use all of the sounds in most adult languages, such as the Arabic and Hebraic 'gutturals' as well as the "clicks" that are unique to primitive languages and that survive in modern languages only as interjections of sorrow, admiration, etc.[1]

The modern, descriptive approach to children's language development, which was widely used during the early twentieth century, is perhaps best exemplified by Dr. Arnold Gesell and his colleagues, who systematically observed children at successive age levels. The following are a few representative descriptions:

44

"Language behavior embraces comprehension as well as communication. The one-year-old infant is not very articulate. Ordinarily he can speak only one or two words in addition to dada and mama and they have slight communication value...

"The two-year-old is burgeoning with words. He may have as many as a thousand. In some instances, however, he may have only a few words at his command. Ordinarily, jargon has almost has almost entirely vanished....

"Questioning is at a peak at Four. A bright four-year-old can elaborate and improvise questions almost endlessly...Sometimes he chatters along to maintain social rapport and to attract attention. He also likes to play on words in a clownish way, particularly if he has an audience."[2]

Like other psychologists of the modern era, Gesell believed not only that language growth was progressive, but also that the patterns he observed were universal and regular. There was, in general, little interest in the differences among young children's language acquisition and its role in their individual development.

It was Jean Piaget who moved us towards a more postmodern understanding of children's language with his attention to the *functions* of young children's language.[3] Piaget recognized that even young children use language for different purposes — to get information, to convey desires, to express emotions and so on. Although Piaget assumed that these functions were common to all children, he nonetheless emphasized the varied and different ways that even young children employed language. In his emphasis upon the particularity of language usage, Piaget was anticipating the postmodern perspective.

It was, however, Noam Chomsky who initiated the postmodern psycholinguistic approach to language development.[4] Although his ideas of "surface and deep grammars" — and his postulation of an "innate learning device" for language — reflect the modern ideas of levels of causality and universality, he nonetheless brought together the fields of language development and linguistics. And for the first time, language development was viewed as the "construction" of grammars and of meanings by individual children. The study of grammars has, however, become less popular in the decades since Chomsky's work first appeared, while the investigation of meaning and verbal understanding has moved to center stage. Meanings, of course, tend to be different, particular, and irregular — in the sense that different children interpret the same word, in part at least, on the basis of their own experience.

This transition from an emphasis on the description of universal patterns to the concentration on particular and often irregular meanings has become an important part of the change in our way of thinking about children's language development and the children themselves. Now, we'll take a more detailed look at how language and its meanings differ between cultures and within cultures.

Language Differences Between Cultures

Our postmodern concern with difference has made us aware of the important variations in the diverse cultural meanings conveyed by any given language, in addition to the differences between specific languages. This awareness provides important insights into children's language development and how it should be supported.

In some countries, for example, language has become a symbol of the nation's uniqueness — indeed, of its cultural superiority. This is particularly true of France, where almost any degradation of the language is looked upon as a slight to the culture as a whole. Perhaps because France lacks a strong constitution (there have been at least sixteen different ones since the revolution), language has become a unifying and identifying aspect of the culture. Just as we in the United States seek to defend our Constitution, the French strive to defend their language. They resist the intrusion of non-French words and are upset when a foreigner does not speak the language well. They would rather it not be spoken at all, if it is not spoken properly.

In other cultures, the association between language and national identity is much weaker, and there is less concern about the intrusion of foreign words or the efforts of non-native speakers to use the language. This is true in Spanish-speaking countries, where the native speakers appreciate the foreigner's efforts to use the language and are not offended by errors of grammar or pronunciation. The same is true in Germany and Scandinavian countries, and in Asian countries, where there is also a general appreciation of those foreigners who make the effort to learn at least the basic "Hello," "Please," and "Thank you" of the language.

These considerations become important for teachers working with students from diverse backgrounds. French-speaking children, for example, may not appreciate a teacher who attempts to use some French words but garbles the pronunciation. Children who speak Spanish, German, Scandinavian, and Asian languages, however, tend to welcome a teacher's effort to learn a few basic words of their language and may even help the teacher to pronounce them properly. This role reversal, with the child teaching the teacher, can be a positive ego-building and status-giving experience for children and support their assimilation into the classroom.

So far, we have talked about the attitudes and values of native speakers towards their own language. Most Americans, however, also share some common reactions to various foreign languages. We tend, for example, to find well-spoken French pleasing to the ear. On the other hand, Eastern European, Asian, and Arabic languages tend to sound unpleasant and are likely to evoke less positive feelings. These sorts of differences also hold true for accents. While we may find a Scottish or Irish brogue charming, as we do the accent of French or German people speaking English, the accents of people from Asia and/or the Middle East are often less pleasing. Although these feelings are a product of the language preferences we have grown up with, we may nonetheless extend our feelings about the accents to those who speak them.

Languages and language accents can, then, become a signal that elicits pre-existing attitudes and values (both positive and negative) towards the speaker, quite independently of that individual's personality and qualities as a person. Some of these attitudes, as we have noted, derive simply from sound preferences for the tone and rhythm of particular languages. Or they may come from other sources as well. Some parents may have been prejudiced against non-native speakers and derisively imitated their accents, leading children to absorb these attitudes without ever thinking about them. A negative experience with a foreign language teacher in junior or senior high school might also color attitudes towards the language and all those who speak it.

Adults and children are human, after all, and such attitudes towards those who speak foreign languages or speak with accents are probably more the rule than the exception. What is important is to appreciate that we are likely to have these values and attitudes, and that we need to understand where they come from. With that appreciation and understanding, we can respond to children from different cultures on the basis of their unique personalities and characters, not their language, and in doing so teach children to do the same.

Language Differences Within Cultures

Even when children of the same age speak the same language, there are differences in accent, pronunciation, and dialect that are associated with values and attitudes. England provides a particularly appropriate example. In contrast to France, where the French language is a unifying force, in England the language

48

can be regarded as divisive, as it separates the social classes. Those who attend public schools (our private schools) and universities speak quite differently than those who do not. Perhaps the most familiar example of this language-related class difference is the story of *My Fair Lady*, in which a British academic attempts to teach a poor young woman with a Cockney accent to speak upper-class English. After changing the way she speaks, she is mistaken for royalty.

To some extent, language serves this purpose in all cultures. Those who are educated tend to speak differently than those who are not, and this is an immediate index of social standing. The relationship between language and social standing is often dramatized in stories of a lower-class individual who has succeeded financially but whose language still lacks refinement, or an educated person who becomes a tramp yet continues to talk like a college graduate.

In addition to social class, language can also serve as an indicator of the region of the country from which one comes. In our country, people growing up in the Mid-west speak what might be called "standard" English, against which other speech is compared. New England accents are quite distinct from Southern accents, which in turn, are different from New York City accents. While prejudices against regional accents are generally less strong than those against social-class language differences, they nonetheless exist and need to be recognized.

Over and above regional differences, there are also many "sub-languages" that are used among one group within the culture but not others. In German, for example, there is "Hoch Deutsche" or High German — which is used on the radio, in advertising and in business and education — and there is "Sprech Deutsche" or speaking German, which is used among friends in less formal situations. A foreigner who understands high German will nonetheless be at a loss when Sprech Deutsche is being used. In the Caribbean, "Pidgin English" is a kind of "patois" or sub-language natives speak when they talk amongst themselves.

In our society, the most common sub-language is Black English, a distinct dialect with its own verb forms (e.g., "I be"), expressions, and vocabulary — and its own cultural significance. In Germany and the Caribbean, the sub-languages are primarily ways of keeping conversations between intimates on a personal rather than formal level, and ways of maintaining privacy in the company of those who do not speak the sub-language. Black English, however, has taken on somewhat the same significance as the French language has for the French. For some African-Americans, Black English is a matter of pride and identity, a way of distinguishing themselves from a larger, hostile white culture. From this perspective, the Blacks who speak standard English may be perceived as having sold out to "the Man."

The values associated with Black English present real problems for those who teach African-American inner city children. Black English does not map well onto standard English — the language of the teacher and of the textbooks and readers. For this reason, a child who speaks Black English is likely to be severely handicapped within our education system. Not only is learning and using standard English more difficult, it is often unacceptable to those peers who regard Black English as a way of maintaining a sense of personal identity. Many African-American children and adults therefore learn to "switch registers" — to speak Black English in some contexts and standard English in others. By providing opportunities for children to speak Black English in the classroom, teachers may find children more willing to learn standard English as well, so long as they are only required to speak it under certain conditions.

Our attitudes towards differences within our own language are usually much more subtle than attitudes towards differences between languages, but they can be equally powerful. As teachers, for example, we are likely to feel more comfortable with children who talk the same way that we do than we do with children who sound different. Obviously, becoming aware of these feelings is the first step towards overcoming them, and this same principle applies to yet another language difference found even within the same class, region or cultural group.

Our postmodern, egalitarian ethos has also alerted us to important differences in the way language is used with and by different genders. For example, it has been shown that parents and teachers speak differently to boys than they do to girls. In our culture, adults tend to use more words relating to feelings and emotions when talking to girls than when talking to boys. And there are also gender-related speech interaction patterns, as boys tend to interrupt girls more than girls interrupt boys. From an early age and for a variety of reasons, boys and girls learn different ways of communicating with one another and with adults. As part of the reinvention of childhood, we adults therefore have to be aware of these differences and to counter their negative aspects wherever possible.

English as a Second Language

Cultural attitudes and images have long had a strong influence on the way we have perceived our language and taught it to children from other cultures. Up until about mid-century, the metaphor of the "melting pot" summed up the prevailing approach. According to this idea, an immigrant could be melted down, mixed with others, poured into a mold, and would re-emerge as a newly minted "Yankee Doodle Dandy." During the modern era, it was simply taken for granted that every immigrant would learn English and eventually forsake his or her native tongue.

Of course, it didn't really work that way. Many immigrant groups printed newspapers in their own languages, had their own theaters and clubs, and created neighborhoods that in many ways resembled the neighborhoods of their homelands. Although these ethnic groups assimilated some aspects of American culture and values, they also perpetuated many of their own.

Even so, there was little formal recognition of the fact that many children entering our schools spoke English as a second language. And because many children did not enter school until they had reached first grade, they had already had a chance to learn English on the streets and from radio and the movies. As a result, most of these children were able to cope in school, and there seemed little need to worry about the fact that these children were bilingual and that English was their second language.

In the postmodern era, we understand that people don't melt and cultures never assimilate fully. There is a new acceptance and valuation of cultural differences, and a greater recognition of the problems faced by children who have grown up hearing and speaking a different language — or two — at home. In addition, the rapid expansion of early childhood education programs, coupled with new waves of immigration, has meant that early childhood educators now have to deal with more children who have English as a second language and who have had less opportunity to pick up English on the street and in play with peers. As a result, many schools now have English-as-a-Second-Language (ESL) programs, bilingual education programs, or both, and there is a conceptual and practical need to deal with the issue of educating children for whom English is a second language.

As travelers in a foreign country, we are likely to feel humbled by young children who are so fluent in the language we are struggling to speak and understand. This experience can help us more fully appreciate the difficulty of learning a foreign language. But back in our own country, we may feel annoyed by a cab driver or service station attendant who speaks broken English, yet who rattles away to a compatriot in what sounds like a totally meaningless babble of sounds. Having forgotten how difficult it is to learn a foreign language — and what a relief it is to talk in our "native tongue" with a compatriot — we may undervalue the achievement of those for whom English is a new means of communication.

Thanks to the work of neurolinguist Eric Lennenburg,[5] it is now generally accepted that second languages are most effectively and easily learned before the twelfth year of life. As a rule, the earlier a child is exposed to a second language, the more easily he or she will learn and retain it. This fact should make us even more appreciative of the efforts of those who are trying to learn English as adults.

In addition to age, however, the other necessary condition for successfully learning a second language is *motivation*. A child who moves to this country from another, or whose parents speak a foreign language at home, will naturally learn his or her parents' language at home, but will learn English outside the home. In both cases, the learning is fueled by strong needs. The child has to acquire the parental language in order to communicate about the basics of everyday life, while outside the home he or she has to master English to get along in school, to meet and make friends, and to successfully navigate the larger community.

A personal example may help to make the importance of motivation in learning and speaking a foreign language more clear. When our first child was two, we moved to French Switzerland for a year so that I could study with Piaget. Our French-Swiss neighbors took care of our child whenever we traveled, and he befriended and played with French-speaking children. As a result, my son learned French very quickly and spoke it without any accent. He even acquired many of the idiomatic expressions used by French-speaking children, such as "cornichon a la creme" (cucumbers and cream), which he said when he burped.

We returned home by ship, and when some American passengers heard him speak French to a waiter, they asked him a question in French. He replied to them in English, because he could tell that they were non-native speakers, and he would not put out the energy to speak French to those who spoke French with an American accent.

53

The issue of motivation in second-language learning is particularly important for early childhood educators. Knowing that young children find it easier to learn a foreign language than do older children and adults, some parents and educators believe early childhood is the best time to teach their child French, Spanish or even Japanese. But while it is certainly true that young children learn a second language easily, it is also true that this only happens when the child has a strong need to learn. Second-language learning and speaking, even for a young child, is hard work, and the child will not put forth all that effort unless he or she has good reason to do so.

Unfortunately, in our society, there is no strong reason for a child to learn any language other than English. Time spent trying to teach young children a foreign language, therefore, is often wasted because the children have no inducement to use the language outside the classroom. Nor is their learning reinforced as it would be if they were living in the country where the foreign language was the operative one. In that case, they would not only listen to it spoken on the street and hear it on television, they would also be required to speak it at least some of the time. Accordingly, unless children in this country have a strong motivational context for learning a foreign language, such instruction often has no lasting benefits. On the other hand, a child who comes to school not knowing English will pick it up quickly, because he or she has such strong motivation to do so.

For teachers, it is very important to give the non-English-speaking child the best possible language model. Although much can be communicated non-verbally, particularly when accompanied by a smile, we should model good standard English wherever possible. When we teach such children the names for things, we need to speak slowly and carefully, and to articulate as clearly as possible. We must also remember that the worst roadblocks for children, as for adults, are slang and colloquial expressions. A child just learning English may have difficulty understanding another child who says, "Do that and you are history." We should try to avoid slang and metaphoric expressions when speaking to ESL children.

The situation is different when a school is located in an area where there is a large ethnic group and where the second language is reflected in the neighborhood stores and newspapers. In such schools, where many or most of the children come to school with English as a second language, a bilingual program may be appropriate. This can be done by having a teacher's aide in the room, who preferably is a native speaker and can teach the English-speaking children the second language at the same time that he or she instructs the non-English speakers. In this kind of setting, English-speaking children will be motivated to learn the foreign language because their peers speak it. Of course, it is very important to have a person who speaks the other language well serve in this capacity, because so much of language learning is based on imitation.

The matter becomes a bit more complex when formal instruction in tool subjects (the three R's) needs to be introduced. Some Canadian studies suggest that children whose first language is French learn to read better if they do so in French rather than in English. To be sure, these children will also learn to read English, but they will master the general reading skills more effectively if they first acquire these skills by learning to read in their primary language.

Here in the United States, this issue is most often encountered with Spanish-speaking children. In some communities, the majority of children have Spanish as their first language and English as their second language. For such children, learning to read in Spanish before learning to read in English may make it easier to acquire this skill. The issue should not be confounded with nationalist concerns about English being the language of the land. Anyone who lives in the United States has to, and will, learn English. The decision about whether to learn to read first in Spanish or in English is a pedagogical, not a political, matter.

Sometimes, when there are a number of children in the class-room who have English as a second language, they may use their first language to exclude others — including teachers — from their conversation. This can be offsetting, but one way of handling it is to organize a time and a place for children to speak their native language. In this way, children can use their mother tongue but also learn that it is appropriate to use the language in some settings and not in others. This is really a matter of good manners and should be taught to children from that perspective, as it is no different than learning that you can shout on the playground but not in the library.

As Americans, we are not always forgiving of those who are struggling to master our language. At such times, we need to recall our own struggles to learn a foreign language and try to become more appreciative of those striving to learn English. We should also value children who come to us speaking languages other than our own, because they have a different outlook on life than we do and can help us to broaden our own perspective. In addition, as these children struggle to learn English, we gain a deeper appreciation of some of the complexities of the language we speak and the difficulties learning English presents for all children. Thus, in many different ways, encounters with people who speak other languages can enrich the classroom and help all of us learn.

Teaching Young Children to Read

One of the clearest examples of our postmodern reinvention of childhood is in our new understanding of how children learn to read. In the modern era, reading was thought of primarily in "stimulus/response" terms. Reading research, for example, concentrated on children's discrimination of letters and words as visual forms, and the translation of such forms into speech sounds. Such an approach assumed that young children learned solely by responding to stimuli, and it led to an extended controversy over reading instruction, with various groups debating whether the "whole word" or "phonics" approaches provided more effective stimuli. In 1958, for example, Rudolf Flesh[6] argued that children were not learning to read because they were not being taught phonics, and forty years later this argument has taken on new life.

Meanwhile, the "Chomsky revolution" has engendered a whole new way of thinking about reading and the abilities children utilize in acquiring it. Chomsky's work encouraged us to look at young children as "seekers after meaning" who were constructing their own grammars and syntax. It also encouraged us to recognize that children's linguistic "errors" were actually evidence of their linguistic knowledge. This all led some authors, such as Kenneth Goodman and Frank Smith, to suggest that reading was, in effect, no different from oral language, and that given an appropriately supportive environment, children could learn to read much as they learn to speak. In the words of Kenneth Goodman:

> "Reading is a language process, the direct counterpart of listening...As long as they get some exposure to written language, most learners will acquire at least a modicum of literacy." [7]

The views of Goodman and Smith[8] gave rise to the "language experience" approach to reading, which, when carried to the extreme, argued that there was no need to regard reading as a new and difficult set of skills that had to be introduced in carefully planned ways with materials designed expressly for that purpose. This approach appealed to educators reacting against the traditional associational methods, which often included books that employed artificial and stilted language (such as the Dick and Jane basal readers mentioned in this book's preface) and did not allow children to use whatever linguistic knowledge they did possess. However, such views played down the very real differences between the contexts of learning that apply to oral and written language.

Today, there is a better appreciation of the very real differences between written and oral language. In particular, while the search for meaning is common to both, the context of learning is quite different for these two means of communication. A child who is making sense of oral speech uses not just the spoken words, but also the whole context of the situation (including the non-verbal communication discussed in the next section of this chapter). In contrast, the words presented in a book have no such contextual support, so the context has to be discovered and constructed by the reader based on his or her earlier experience.

There are other important differences as well, such as the role of motivation. Oral language can be highly motivational, both in a positive and negative sense, as when children are being praised or cautioned not to do something, told about upcoming pleasurable events such as holidays, and so on. Children themselves are motivated to use oral language to express desires, pleasures and pains. Print, on the other hand, like a foreign language, is emotionless and has nothing to stimulate the child's interest and emotions, until the child can read well enough to find meaning in it.

Further, the interactions between the child and the printed page are also different than oral interactions in other ways. Not only are the motivations and feelings during a conversation more immediate and accessible, but also the child can ask for the information to be repeated or explained. And a parent or teacher can take the initiative in assisting a child who they see is having difficulty comprehending or replying. There is no such give and take with a text. The child may ask a question, but the text does not answer; the reader may be confused, but the text does not amplify or clarify itself.

In all these ways, learning to read is a very different process than learning to talk, even though they share the search for meaning. Contemporary educators are therefore using a more balanced approach to teach children to read. Some of the contributions of what has come to be called the "whole language" approach remain important, such as the ideas that reading is part of language and that the more children speak, are read to, and write their own stories, the easier it will be for them to master written language. But at the same time, learning to read is also supported by a well-thought-out sequence of instructional practices, along with carefully constructed or chosen materials. In an appropriately postmodern way, we recognize that reading instruction can and should involve not only a rich exposure to all facets of language, but also the learning of sight words and phonics.

Another seemingly recent innovation, which was actually introduced by Maria Montessori, is that children should "write first, read later." This is a complete reversal of the modern dictum that children should "read first, write later," and in modern times many people knew how to read but were unable to write. Montessori recognized, however, that when children put wooden letters together to form words, it facilitated the reading process. Today, thanks to computers, children can type out words before they can write with pen or pencil. And when writing, young children are encouraged to engage in "inventive spelling" in order to get their thoughts out on paper without worrying about whether or not words are spelled correctly, so that the children can find meaning in their writing and develop the motivation that will help them learn to spell well at a later age. For these and other reasons, writing and reading now are most often taught concurrently.

A final postmodern note about learning to read is the recognition that different children approach reading in their own, different ways. In the book, *Growing Up With Language*, Naomi Baron[9] reports on three children who each found their own path to literacy. Ryan found the whole word approach most comfortable and recognized a wide number of words — from the names of his peers on their "cubbies" to a number of words in his favorite *Babar* books. Alex not only learned sight words but also began to sound out letters to find out what particular words were. He combined the phonics and whole word approaches, while

Sara took yet a different tack. She memorized whole blocks of text and could "read" a book by reciting the text by heart and knowing just when to turn the page. In sum, we now recognize that there is no one universally "best" path to reading; instead, different children need to be given the opportunities to learn in the way that is best for them.

With this in mind, it is also worth noting that parents can support healthy language development in many different ways. Talking to children, even as infants, supports language growth. And as children begin to speak, listening becomes as important as talking. Young children are extraordinarily keen observers and have wonderfully creative language, so if we encourage children to talk, and we listen and respond to what they say, we contribute to language acquisition in a vitally important way. Finally, reading children poetry, stories, and factual articles furthers their language development and prepares them to become active, enthusiastic readers.

Teachers can support and encourage young children's language growth in similar ways. Having circle meetings at the beginning of the day and giving each child a turn to tell about something interesting in his or her life encourages good speaking and listening habits. And when children are in conflict over some material or activity, allowing each child to explain his or her point of view is a good way of resolving the conflict and encouraging language skills at the same time. In addition, when children are at some interesting place for a visit, like a museum, talking about what they see is more important than being quiet.

Non-verbal Communication

When modern psychologists studied language differences between age groups, they largely ignored the non-verbal communications that always accompany oral language. Linguists, however, were always concerned with such communications, and when child development and linguistics were joined together to become psycholinguistics, the interest in non-verbal communication among children was a natural consequence. And as we shall see, non-verbal communication tends to make our use of language more different and particular, rather than universal and regular.

Whenever two or more people are engaged in face-to-face interaction, a great deal of information is being communicated in addition to that transmitted by the words being spoken. For example, if we ask a child to do a chore, saying something such as, "Please erase the board," and the child says, "Oh, sure," with a smile, this means something different than if the child says, "Oh, sure," with a grimace. Thus, body language is another form of communication that needs to be considered along with the use of words. Facial expressions, gestures, and posture all communicate attitudes and feelings that elaborate on the language being used. It is therefore as important to read a child's body language as it is to understand his or her spoken words, keeping in mind that body language can have different meanings depending on the particular situation.

Some types of non-verbal communications, such as traditional gestures, are more or less standard within a culture. In our society, nodding your head up and down indicates agreement, while shaking it from side to side signifies disagreement. Thumbs up usually indicates a positive reaction to an event, whereas thumbs down usually means a negative outcome. Shrugging one's shoulders to signify "I don't know" and shaking one's head in amazement are still other conventional non-verbal communications. Obviously, some non-verbal communications are obscene, and unfortunately children seem to learn these as quickly or more quickly than they learn some of the others. As adults, we need to make it clear to children that such gestures have no place in the classroom.

Certain body language messages that convey children's emotional state are also somewhat standard, even as they reveal how children differ from one another and respond to particular

61

situations. Children who continually fidget, swing their legs while seated, or bite their nails indicate a state of nervousness and/or mild anxiety. Likewise, the child who speaks in a very low tone of voice, hardly above a whisper, may feel frightened, embarrassed, or simply shy.

Sometimes, a child's non-verbal communication may indicate a sensory disability. Children with visual limitations may place their heads too close to the material they are working on, while hearing problems are suggested by a child who always inclines his or her head towards the speaker.

Young children also use body language to tell adults when they want to be close or when they need a hug. In my visits to early childhood classrooms, I usually sit against the wall on a small chair or on the floor. Often, several children, usually boys, will cluster around me and gradually move closer until they are touching my leg. With this cue, I feel comfortable in putting my arm around the child's shoulder. Other children never move close and would be startled — even offended or frightened — if I attempted to put my arm around them. In these situations children should always make the first moves. It is their call as to whether or not they want physical contact, as some children need more personal space than others.

Young children have not learned to conceal their feelings, so their body language is particularly important. With their expressions, gestures and body movements, they tell us much more than they ever could express with words about their particular states of mind.

Chapter 4

Reinventing Socialization

The modern invention of childhood was further defined by the concept of social roles — the idea that people who have a particular social status behave in order to conform to the expectations others have regarding that status. Every individual within a society plays many different social roles that help to determine his or her behavior. For example, a woman in our postmodern society may act as an employee, a supervisor of other employees, a mother, a wife, and a daughter of aging parents —all within the same few hours — and therefore behave differently in each role.

During the modern era, social roles were regarded as the major vehicle of socialization — the process of adapting to a society. It was, however, only with the introduction of universal public schooling in the early nineteenth century that all children were assigned the same unique social role, that of a student. This distinctive role was emphasized by the dressing of children differently than adults, often in school uniforms. And childhood thus came to be defined as a period when schooling was the child's primary occupation. This also made the difference between childhood and adulthood clear, with childhood being a time for schooling and adulthood a time for work.

The perception of social roles during the modern era reflected the basic assumptions of that period, namely, the beliefs in progress, universality, and regularity. Some sociologists (e.g., Parsons, 1949) believed that as society progressed, social roles became more specific and this made society more efficient.[1] Roles were also regarded as universal in the sense that one could find the roles of government official, doctor, business person, and religious leader in every society. And roles were regular in the sense that the expectations for any given role were the same regardless of the individual who played the role.

As we move into the postmodern era, social roles appear both too broad and too narrow to define the socialization process.[2] Socialization is now seen not so much as the progressive acquisition of social roles, but rather as the somewhat random acquisition of the implicit rules, understandings, and expectations that govern our behavior in repetitive social situations. Erving Goffman described these situations as *frames* when they were cultural, and we may call them *scripts* when they are familial.[3] Waiting in line, for example, is a cultural frame, whereas the manner in which we celebrate birthdays tends to be a familial script. Frames and scripts are the "warp and woof" of our social life, regulating our conduct in all those repetitive situations that we tend to take for granted and that Goffman referred to as the "dust of human existence."

Our modern role-based conception of childhood socialization now needs to be reinvented to incorporate the wide range of frames and scripts that today's young children acquire and bring with them to school. The inclusion of frames and scripts within our conception of childhood allows us to value, appreciate, and attend to the attitudes and beliefs of children from different cultural and familial backgrounds. In this chapter, we will first look at the nature of frames and scripts in general, then at how they have changed from the modern to the postmodern era, and finally at how they vary among children from different backgrounds.

Frames

The Variety of Frames

Frames regulate our behavior in virtually all of our social interactions. And despite their variety, frames have so much in common they can be defined by their general characteristics. For the purposes of this book, I will limit the discussion to those frames that are operative in the home and classroom.

There are, first of all, *situational* frames — rules and expectations that regulate children's behavior in specific places. At home, for example, there are kitchen frames, bedroom frames, and family-room frames. At school, there are frames that regulate behavior in the classroom, in the halls, in the library, on the playground, in the lunchroom, and in the principal's office.

Children quickly acquire the rules of these situational frames. At home, they learn that clothes are to be left in the bedroom, not in the kitchen or family room. Likewise, food is usually eaten in the kitchen or dining room, not in the bedroom. At school, even at the kindergarten level, children develop and demonstrate an understanding of the fact that they must be quiet in the library but not on the playground.

Children also use a number of *people* frames that are usually signaled by "tag terms" such as "Uncle Marty," "nerd," or "substitute teacher," all of which provoke predictable reactions. At school, there are many *curriculum* frames such as the rules, expectations and understandings that regulate interactions involving science, social studies, reading, art, dramatic play, and math activities. Finally, we can also observe *travel* frames whenever children go on family outings or school trips to a museum, a wildlife preserve, or other educational settings.

Although the general nature of frames has remained much the same from the modern to the postmodern era, there have been some major changes. This is particularly true for adult/child frames. In the modern era, young children spent

65

most of their lives at home in the care of their mother and father. Today, a majority of young children spend at least part of their lives in out-of-home settings and in the care of non-parental adults. As a result, from an early age, many postmodern children learn to deal with non-parental adults. In addition, because they are with other children of the same age, they also learn child-child "mutuality" frames that they might not have learned in a family with children of different ages. In some ways, therefore, postmodern children are socialized earlier and more broadly than were young children of the modern era.

Teaching Frames

Parents teach frames all of the time. The going-to-bed frame, for example, often involves putting on pajamas, washing and brushing teeth, perhaps reading a story, and then a good-night kiss. Young children come to expect these frames and are upset if they are not followed exactly. To teach frames effectively, parents are best advised to establish clear frames when children are young. Setting firm limits about what children can and cannot do in certain situations is critical in enabling children to incorporate these frames in their lives and abide by them automatically.

Manners serve as a good example of the frames children need to learn early. Parents and teachers should always encourage young children to say "please," "thank you," and "excuse me" in appropriate situations. And parents and teachers teach these frames best if they use good manners themselves, especially with the children in their care, because young children learn politeness frames much more easily when the adults around them "practice what they preach."

During the first half of the twentieth century, children learned classroom frame rules fairly easily, because these rules were often extensions of similar rules, understandings and expectations that the children had already learned at home. Hur-

66

ried and distracted postmodern parents, however, seem to have less time to teach frame rules than did their modern counterparts. And child-care providers may not have the knowledge or authority needed to teach these rules effectively to young children. Today, therefore, we can no longer expect most children to come to our schools having learned the basic adult/child frame rules that are presupposed for children to successfully adapt to classroom settings.

At school, most teachers understand that frame rules are learned most effectively when they are established at the beginning of the academic year, at the onset of the school day, or at the start of a new activity. By introducing the rules right at the beginning and then repeating them occasionally, teachers help children progressively internalize the rules and learn to behave accordingly. Once children become involved in a particular activity, it is often too late to introduce the general frame rules and to get children to abide by them. Put differently, it is much harder to make children stop doing something than it is to keep them from engaging in the activity in the first place.

Throughout their educational experience, children can continue to make use of some of the classroom frames that we instill in them at an early age. Raising your hand to ask a question is a frame that operates at all stages of the educational progression and holds, as well, for participation in adult meetings. Other frames, however, may be unique to a particular instructor in a particular classroom. Some teachers, for example, may utilize cooperative learning and encourage their students to work together on their math or science lessons. Other teachers may insist upon each child doing his or her own work. Both frames are limited to the particular classroom setting and are usually signaled by the teacher's verbal instructions.

Although children learn frames from teachers and other adults, frame rules are often maintained by peer reinforcement. Children, no less than adults, react negatively to a child who is not following the frame rules of the ongoing activity. If, for example, a child fails to wait his turn to use the computer, then the other children will complain loudly to the teacher. Much the same process occurs when adults try to prevent a driver — who has been violating the frame rules by driving on the shoulder of a highway in order to get ahead of slow-moving traffic — from getting back into the regular lane. When anyone breaks a frame rule, peers tend to let him or her know it, and this is a powerful socializing force.

Frame Dynamics

As in situations like the one just described, frame rules are not all-powerful and inviolate, but rather are dynamic and subject in some respects to human activities and interactions. Children, perhaps even more than adults, may understand the frames but, for one or another reason, not behave according to the frame rules and expectations. When frames are not completed satisfactorily due to this or other causes, we speak of *spoiled* frames. In addition, there are many cases where children learn different frame rules at home than those established in the classroom. When this happens we can observe frame *clashes*. And when people become very involved in a particular frame, it can be wrenching to leave that frame and enter into a different one. This is the problem of frame *switches*. One last but very important issue has to do with helping children *modify* frames that may be inappropriate in a particular setting. All these different types of frame dynamics need to be understood as part of our reinvention of childhood.

Spoiled Frames

Frames are not just a set of intellectual rules, expectations, and understandings, they also have an emotional plot or rhythm. That is to say, frames usually have a beginning, middle, and end that comprise a complete story line of feelings, from arousal to resolution. When this feeling pattern is disrupted and the emotions aroused are not expended, the frame is effectively spoiled. Sometimes, this pattern of feelings is upset by something other than the participants themselves. In other situations, a participant spoils the frame accidentally or deliberately breaks the frame rules. Teachers and parents need to be prepared for all these eventualities.

We have all undergone the interruption of an emotional frame by external events. A good example is the spoiling of a "farewell" frame, when, for instance, you have taken some loved ones to the airport and are anticipating your tearful response to the moment of separation. Just as you are prepared to give the last hug and the tears are about to flow, you hear an announcement that the plane has been indefinitely delayed. The frame has been spoiled by events over which you have no control, and it takes you a little while to regain your composure and adapt to the altered circumstances, which create a new frame.

In a similar way, classroom frames can be spoiled by unexpected events. At a school that I once ran in Rochester, New York, a young man once came into the building and stole a leather purse from the secretary's desk in the entrance foyer. The police were called and soon filled our yard with their cars, flashing lights, and sirens. The thief was caught, handcuffed, and then taken away in one of the police cars. All the while, the children were watching the proceedings from the classroom windows, and the learning frames in which they had been engaged were spoiled beyond repair. Following a variation of the adage that "if you can't beat them, join them," we decided to use the episode as the theme for a composition. We had children write their impressions of the event and illustrate these impressions with drawings. This helped the children discharge the new emotions aroused by the unexpected event.

Classroom frames are often spoiled by unexpected events like the one described above. There are fire drills, visits by various dignitaries, power failures, and much, much more. In most instances, it is possible to resume the frame at some later point. On other occasions, as in the example from our own school, it may be best to institute a new frame to take care of the fresh emotions engendered by the intruding event itself. The important thing is to recognize that classroom activities have emotional rhythms, and that when these are disrupted, we have to take some actions to bring them to completion. This kind of frame repair work is especially important when something happens to one of the children in the group. When a child is hurt or becomes seriously ill, his or her fellow classmates need to talk, write, and illustrate some of their feelings and concerns. Likewise, when a group is disrupted by the departure (to another city or state) of one of the children, the feelings aroused by the child's absence have to be addressed.

As previously noted, frames can also be spoiled by those who unintentionally or deliberately violate the frame rules, understandings, and expectations. I have already suggested that when this happens, there is usually a social reaction that is meant to bring the offender back into the frame or to punish him or her. If such a resolution does not occur, however, the emotions are not discharged and may persist well after the frame itself is no longer operative. It is because unresolved frame emotions stay with us that we are more likely to remember an unfinished task — or an unsatisfactory social exchange — than we are a completed task or satisfactory social interaction.

Every teacher and parent is familiar with the power of unresolved emotions left over from spoiled frames. Consider, for example, the familiar "question and answer" classroom frames, in which teachers ask questions and children answer them. Usually, the rules for this frame are that the children will raise their hands if they think they know the answer, and that the teacher will be fair in calling upon different children for the answers. In addition, it is also expected that the teacher will be gentle with those unhappy children who do not know the answer or who give wrong answers. In such frames, children expect that they

70

will be treated fairly — that if they give the right answer, they will be rewarded, and if not, nothing especially bad will happen to them.

Now, suppose that during a particular question and answer frame, a teacher slips up (as we all do at times) and dismisses a child's wrong answer with, "No, that's not it at all. Why don't you pay attention?" With this response he or she has *spoiled* the frame in the sense that the teacher has reinforced, rather than assuaged, the child's bad feelings. Later in the day, the child whose answer was so curtly dismissed may "accidentally" knock over the teacher's coffee cup. This completes the emotional cycle left unfinished by the teacher's response.

Another familiar frame that is often spoiled is that of choosing children to perform special duties such as erasing the blackboard or distributing snacks. The basic frame rule for this activity is that the teacher will be fair and that the children will abide by his or her selections. If, inadvertently, the teacher chooses a particular child twice in a row or consistently more often than the other children, the remaining youngsters give evidence of their displeasure either by misbehavior or by directly challenging the teacher's fairness. A frame rule has been broken, and children will not be satisfied until some restorative action, such as choosing a different child, has been taken.

Sometimes, of course, it is the pupil, not the teacher, who effectively spoils a frame. During a reading or a math activity, a particular child may get up and wander about the room, making noise and distracting others. Some of the other children may complain to the teacher or to the disrupting child. Group pressure may suffice to settle the child down, or the teacher may have to intervene and reassert the frame rules.

Some children, usually those with emotional problems, may not subordinate themselves to the frame rules. Knowing that obeying the rules ensures group acceptance and breaking them insures group rejection, some children act so as to invite such rejection. That is to say, some children break the frame rules not because they do not know what the frame rules are, but rather because they do know them and welcome the classroom disruption their behavior elicits.

When a child spoils a frame, therefore, it is necessary to determine whether the child simply does not know what the frame rules are, or whether he or she is breaking them deliberately. If the child does not know the frame rules, then it is appropriate to verbalize these rules for him or her. On the other hand, if the child knows the rules and breaks them intentionally, we might remove the child from the frame by taking the child to a quiet place and engaging him or her in some other activity, before allowing him or her to re-enter it at another time.

It is also true that some children break the frame rules not to get attention, but because they are unable to control their own behavior. An example might be children suffering from ADHD (Attention Deficit/Hyperactivity Disorder). This syndrome, which can result from any combination of one or more neurological, physiological, psychological, or sociological risk factors, may make it almost impossible for a child to learn and to follow frame rules. In our postmodern world, we are seeing many more children who act this way than we ever saw in the past, but it is always important that such a child receives a full and careful evaluation to ensure that he or she is indeed ADHD, rather than a child who has been inadequately socialized at home.

Frame Clashes

A child or teacher who comes from a cultural background that is different from that of the majority of the students often brings along a set of frames that differ from those that are already in play within the classroom. In such situations, we have a frame clash, like one I witnessed when visiting a school attended by a number of Navaho children in New Mexico.

In the Navaho culture, looking is a very powerful activity and is framed in a variety of ways. When entering a wickiup (tepee), for example, children are taught to look down and around before looking up. Navaho youngsters are also trained not to stare at a brother or sister when he or she is not clothed. Perhaps most importantly, Navaho children are admonished from an early age not to look adults in the eyes when they speak to them. Children who make such eye contact are regarded as being disrespectful and ill-mannered.

What I witnessed in the Navaho school was a frame clash between the Navaho children and a new teacher who had just graduated from a university on the East Coast. In a course on troubled children, she had learned that autistic children (those with a severe emotional dysfunction that appears early in life and is manifested by lack of social responsiveness to the point of treating people like objects) never look in the eyes of people who are talking to them. This young teacher had also been taught that her first task when working with young children was to make eye contact, because only in that way would she be able to get their attention and teach them.

Having come to teach Navaho children in a Head Start program on a reservation, her first meeting with the children was an enormous shock. Not a single child looked her in the eye, and she became concerned that she had been assigned an entire class of autistic children! When she insisted that they look her in the eyes, the children felt embarrassed and resisted. They were also deeply conflicted because they assumed that they would be punished if they looked at her, and punished if they did not. So, they glanced up quickly and then down again. Fortunately, a supervisor who knew Navaho culture was on the scene and drew the teacher aside to explain the children's frame to her.

A Head Start teacher in Lowell, Massachusetts gave me another example. Many Cambodian children participate in her program, and the behavior of one boy puzzled her. At lunchtime, he would routinely knock some of the food off of his plate and then dutifully clean it up and throw it in the trash. She later learned from a Cambodian teacher that it is very impolite in Cambodian society not to eat everything on your plate. The boy was routinely given more food than he could eat but felt he could not refuse it, so he conveniently knocked what he did not want onto the floor, knowing he would not be expected to eat it. This was his ingenious way to resolve a frame clash.

I believe that many of the difficulties teachers have with children from different ethnic backgrounds result from just such frame clashes — where neither of the participants understands the other's underlying frames. African-American children, for example, use their bodies as well as words to communicate. Much of the touching, jostling, and nudging these children engage in is not hostile or intrusive, but rather constitutes an intricate form of non-verbal communication. For the most part, white people limit their communications to words and facial expressions, so it is easy for white teachers to misinterpret African-American children's motor behavior, and it is equally easy for African-American children to misinterpret a white teacher's communication. (From the African-American frame perspective, lack of body language gives evidence of emotional stiffness and being "uptight.")

Some cultural frame clashes also occur because children come with different learning styles than those that are common to the host culture and school. At the school I mentioned earlier, we served children whom I called "curriculum disabled." These were youngsters of average ability who were performing below the academic norm at a public school. They attended our school full-time, and in addition to classroom work, they were individually tutored by college undergraduates for whom this work counted as a course credit. After a year or two, most of the children were able to return to the public school working at or above grade level.

One student who came to our school was an eight-year-old boy named Ross. He came from Jamaica, where the schools had been set up by the English and emphasized rote learning. By endorsing rote learning — through which children learn the form but not the substance of things — colonial powers were able to keep their subjects from engaging in critical thinking, and to ensure that the populace would passively obey rules that were not in their own self-interest. Ross, who had been schooled in this way, wanted to learn everything by rote. It took us a year to get him to use other strategies, such as trial-and-error and hypothesis testing.

Even children from the same socioeconomic and ethnic background may experience frame clashes, if they come from another state or even from a different school. Every classroom quickly establishes a number of frames that are unique to that classroom, and to which a new student must be introduced. To take a simple example, a child attending school in Cincinnati had been allowed to get up and to leave the classroom in his own way when the bell rang at the end of the day. Then, after a family move to another part of the city, he entered another school at mid-year. The teachers there had established a frame in which the children stood up and left in alphabetical order, according to their last names. After a few false starts, the child quickly mastered this new leaving-the-room frame.

Frame Switches

A somewhat different frame disruption arises when the child is unable to switch — or switch rapidly enough — from one frame to another. I observed such an instance in a kindergarten class, when the teacher said, "Children, put your things away and line up at the door; it's time to go outside." A boy named George, who was making a clay animal, continued to work on his project. The teacher asked, "George, didn't you hear what I said?" George replied, "Yes," and continued working on his clay animal. The teacher recognized that she had given him

75

enough warning and said, "Okay George, take a few more minutes to finish your model and then join us outside."

In general, frame switches are difficult for both children and adults. If we are relaxing on a Sunday, reading the papers in old clothes, we will probably be reluctant to accept an invitation to dinner that requires us to get dressed up. We might like to go to dinner, but we don't want to switch frames. Likewise, children may be very reluctant to go to summer camp but love camp once they get there. Once at camp, moreover, they are often reluctant to come home. Once we like the frames we are in, we don't like to change, so frame switching is always a struggle.

Experienced teachers understand the importance of letting children know well in advance that a frame switch is going to take place. And the younger the children, the more advance notice they require. One teacher I observed, a former airline stewardess, prepared her children for going home by saying, "We are going to land in fifteen minutes. I want papers, crayons, and books stowed for landing." She also recognized that children needed to be reminded more than once that a frame switch is in the offing, and so repeated her announcement several more times.

There are many other time-limit metaphors ("half-time is almost over," "the train will be coming into the station," etc.) that adults can use to prepare children to switch frames. Whatever words or metaphor we use, the important thing is that we prepare children well in advance of the time when they will be changing to a new activity with its own rules, expectations, and understandings. It is also true that the more complicated or personal the frame, the more difficult it is to switch. Divorce, so common in our postmodern world, is a very wrenching frame switch, particularly for children. If we know such an event is going to happen, we need to encourage parents to talk with their children about all the changes that will come about, to help prepare them for this emotionally devastating re-arrangement of their lives.

Modifying Frames

In this diverse and dynamic postmodern society, adults need to be prepared to modify frames that are inappropriate. This issue raises many social and moral issues, over and above a consideration of the psychological mechanisms. In general, modifying a child's classroom frames is the simplest task and usually has few moral or ethical consequences, because these frames are not deeply rooted and children usually have no abiding emotional investment in them. Children can learn to work cooperatively after having learned to work individually, and vice versa.

However, when we set out to modify social, cultural, or ethnic frames that clash with those of the school, the situation becomes more complicated, as in the following example. It happened while I was observing day care centers in Germany, which at that time had relatively large numbers of Turkish children — the offspring of Turkish men who had been brought in to work in the German factories. During snack time at one center I visited, a young boy who looked to be about four years old knocked over his glass of milk as he reached over to get a cracker. The teacher gave him a paper towel and asked him to wipe up the milk he had spilled. The boy adamantly refused. The teacher was obviously taken aback but insisted, and the boy finally wiped up the spill with an angry, disgusted expression. I learned later that on the following day, the boy's irate father came to the school and told the teacher that she must never again ask his son to clean up the table, because in the Turkish culture cleaning up was women's (and girls') work.

This is clearly a delicate situation. The child brings his cultural frame to the classroom, and it is in clear conflict with the frames established by the teacher, as well as the larger society. What is the teacher to do? If he or she insists on changing the child's frame, the teacher is, in effect, challenging the child's culture and parent. On the other hand, if the teacher does not enforce the frame rule — that every child is to clean up his or her

77

own mess — the other children will feel that the teacher is being unfair, and so will experience a spoiled frame.

One option in this situation is to use the event to teach children about cultural diversity. The teacher might explain to the children that in the culture from which this child's parents come, men do not do the cleaning. In discussing the issue, the teacher might suggest that this should not be viewed simply as a matter of right and wrong or good and bad, it is *different* and we need to understand and respect this difference even if we do not agree with it. At the same time, the Turkish child needs to understand and respect the rules and customs of the society and the school in which he now spends his time.

By discussing the matter in this way, the teacher provides a natural and spontaneous lesson in how different cultures are, even in regard to simple, everyday occurrences. By allowing children to express their culture and by acknowledging this frame with sympathy and understanding, we set a very positive example of our own appreciation of cultural and ethnic diversity.

Before ending this discussion of frames modification, it is necessary to say something about modifying *dysfunctional* frame behavior. Dysfunctional frame behavior is individual rather than social, cultural, or ethnic, and it often occurs when children create their own frames for dealing with unhappiness or frustration. For example, in the school I ran, I had a child who would hit other children whenever he felt they had blocked or interfered with his ongoing activity. The staff would always restrain him from hitting other children and encourage him to show his anger verbally rather than by hitting.

On one occasion, I actually had to hold his arms at his sides to keep him from throwing a chair at another child. Eventually, however, he was able to translate his "hitting-when-frustrated" frame into a "talking-when-frustrated" frame. In fact, he learned this verbal response to frustration perhaps a bit too well. One day, as I was leaving the school for a dental appointment, I said to him,

"Ron, I am sure you will be happy to hear that I am going to the dentist." Without raising his head from his work, he replied, "I hope you have a thousand cavities." Ron now had an effective verbal frame for dealing with his angers and resentments.

Scripts

Our postmodern reinvention of childhood must also include a new appreciation of differences that are unique to families and that cut across cultural, ethnic, and racial divisions. While the modern image of childhood assumed that all children came from comparable nuclear families, today we recognize the wide variety of family forms in which children are being reared. An understanding of family scripts helps us to deal more effectively with individual families and the children who are part of them.

Families, for example, differ in the manner in which they celebrate birthdays, in the ways in which they regard illnesses, in their acceptance of foul language, and even with respect to personal property. Parents also differ in their beliefs regarding which scripts to follow as parents. Obviously, when children bring family scripts about matters such as these to the classroom, they can be a source of spoiled frames and frame clashes.

Birthday Scripts

Take the matter of birthdays. For some parents, this is an occasion to bake cookies and cupcakes for all the children in the class, and to have a cake with candles that can be lit at snack time. Other parents may not feel that this is necessary, may not have the time to do the preparation, or may not be able to afford the expense of the treats. A child whose parents, for whatever reason, do not want to provide cake and cookies for the entire class, may well feel embarrassed and ashamed when it is his or her birthday and no special goodies are available. Some classmates might even taunt the child about it.

79

As a teacher, you have several options. One is simply to exclude any parental birthday offerings. Of course, it is important to explain to parents the reason for this (to prevent embarrassment to the other children whose parents cannot provide in this way). Another option is to request from the school a small budget for birthdays, so that all the children can have a special treat without parental involvement. A third option is to treat this as a kind of culture clash and explain to the children that some families place a great deal of emphasis upon birthdays while others do not. When possible, the second option is probably the best, as every child's birthday gets celebrated in the same way.

Illness Scripts

Illness is another type of family script that can be a cause of conflict. In some families, illness is something bad that happens to you through no fault of your own. If it happens, you are allowed to stay home from work or from school, and you are catered to a bit. You may be given hot tea with lemon if you have a cold, and you may even be allowed to watch the "soaps" during the afternoon. In a family such as this, illness provides an opportunity to show tender, loving care.

In other families, however, illness is not something that happens to you; it is something that *you* let happen to you — and that you should not have let happen. Illness represents weakness and giving in, which is not acceptable behavior. In this sort of family, therefore, you go to school or to work no matter how bad you feel.

Clearly, these different family scripts can and do lead to classroom conflicts. When a child from a "tough-it-out family" comes to school with a cold, other parents who subscribe to the tender-loving-care script of illness may say that the child with a cold should stay home, both for his or her sake and so as not to infect the other children. In this instance, the teacher is caught between two family scripts, neither of which is necessarily right or wrong, but which are nonetheless quite different.

Under these circumstances, the teacher may have to mediate between two parental scripts, knowing that the situation may be complicated by other factors, as well. Some parents who might want to keep a sick child home may be unable to do so, due to a combination of child-care and financial reasons. Although some companies now have sick-leave policies for parent employees, many do not, so too many parents are still penalized if they choose to stay home with a sick child.

In the best of all worlds, early childhood programs would have areas set aside for sick children. Unfortunately, very few early childhood or school settings actually have such facilities. So, one strategy for educators is to establish a policy regarding sick children and require all parents to accept it if they wish to enroll the child in the program. This makes parents think ahead to the likelihood of illnesses occurring and arrange in advance for such an eventuality.

Of course, a remaining difficulty is determining just when a child is ill. A child who has the mumps or the measles may be most contagious before the symptoms appear. Likewise, it is not always clear whether a child who has a slight cold should be kept home from school day after day. In reality, no matter how hard we try, there will be situations where a contagious child is in the classroom, and this has to be explained to parents as well. It is an inescapable fact that children who spend their weekdays in child-care facilities, preschools and elementary schools will experience more illness than those who do not. The positive side is that they also build up more immunities, in addition to receiving the other benefits these sorts of educational settings can provide.

Foul Language Scripts

Another family scripting issue that can cause clashes in the classroom has to do with swearing and foul language. In some families, the use of such language is commonplace, and the children pick it up easily and proceed to use it in the classroom. Other parents, who maintain homes in which such language is seldom if ever used, hear their children use words that make them quite unhappy and complain to the teacher about the language the child is bringing home. Usually, parents believe that it is the teacher's responsibility to outlaw such language.

This problem is particularly acute in the postmodern world, where television, videos, and explicit lyrics often influence young people. Even children in protected homes often hear and say words that their parents might not have even known and certainly would never have uttered. Unfortunately, obscene gestures may also be part of the postmodern child's repertoire, although he or she may have little or no understanding of the gestures' meaning. All these trends have made family language scripts much more of an intrusive issue than they were in the modern era.

Of course, the problem is that teachers cannot be everywhere at once, particularly with twenty-five or more students. And it is especially difficult for a teacher to monitor children's language on the playground or when children are engaged in small group activities. In response to parents who are upset about this issue, we must explain that we are equally troubled by it and that we handle it by telling the child or children that we don't want to hear that language. We need to encourage parents to respond in a similar way, but we must also remind parents that while we wish it were otherwise, children are going to hear this language from peers, on television, at the movies, and even on the radio. This does not excuse its being used in the classroom, but as elsewhere in the society, it has become more commonplace and difficult to control.

Personal Property Scripts

A somewhat different clash often develops as a result of different family scripts regarding personal property. In some families, children are taught from an early age to respect other people's things and not to touch or use them without permission. If children are given permission to use them, the objects must be treated with care and respect. Other families, however, do not share this orientation. In such families, everyone uses everything in a somewhat communal fashion, so there is much less attachment to personal belongings. Unfortunately, this diminished sense of ownership may also make family members lax about caring for things outside the home.

These opposing family scripts can become a source of conflict and unhappiness in the classroom. A child who comes from a "respect-for-personal-property" family may bring a toy to school to show to the other children. Without warning, a child from a family in which everything is communal grabs the toy and plays with in a rough fashion, so that it breaks. The child who has brought the toy is very upset, not only because the toy was used and broken, but also because the other child never even asked to use it. In this situation, the teacher must establish a frame rule for the class, stating that no one must use someone else's possession without asking, and everyone must use another person's possession with care. It is also reasonable for the teacher to tell the parents of the child who broke the toy what happened and explain that it would be a nice gesture if they replaced it.

Disciplinary Scripts

A related family scripting issue has to do with discipline. In some homes, children are slapped or hit as a means of control and discipline. Aggression, however, begets aggression, and when that child comes to school, he or she is likely to hit other children. Naturally, parents who believe it is wrong to hit children become quite upset when they learn that their child has been hit, punched, or kicked at school. As teachers, we can only say that we are very sorry and do our best to control such behavior, and that we make clear to the offending child with every means we have that such behavior is totally unacceptable. Depending on the situation, we can also say that we have told the parents that unless they can help the child control his or her behavior, the child will have to leave the program. Aggression, beyond the normal limits of childhood fights, should not be tolerated in the classroom or on the playground.

Unfortunately, aggressive behavior is much more common among today's young children than it was among children growing up in the modern era. One reason is that postmodern youngsters have much to be upset and angry about. Many have parents who have separated or divorced, or who have such busy schedules that there is little time for sustained, enjoyable interactions. Also, some children may be upset — or influenced in other ways — by some of the violence and mayhem that is so endemic on TV. And they may be stressed by the long hours they have to spend away from their own homes. We cannot undo all these sources of anger and resentment, but we can recognize that this aggression is a reaction to life circumstances and not necessarily the expression of an angry personality. And we need to do all that we can to provide young children with a less stressful and violence-prone environment.

Parenting Scripts

A somewhat different clash of family scripts directly reflects the contrast between modern and postmodern perceptions of parenting. Some parents continue to feel strongly that it is their responsibility to stay home and look after their children, even though they might prefer to be out pursuing an exciting career. Other parents have accepted the postmodern sentiment of shared parenting and believe that they are better parents because they are realizing their abilities and talents, as well as earning needed money.

Both parenting scripts can be quite successful, and both can be failures. This depends primarily on the parent's attitude (usually it is the mother who stays home, but there are also househusbands who stay home to care for the children). If the parent is doing what he or she really wants to do — stay home or work — he or she will probably be a better parent than if he or she is doing something that goes against the grain. In short, parents who feel good about themselves will do a better job of parenting than one who does not.

Another problem arises when parents with opposing scripts have children in the same class and school. A principal in a school system just outside New York City told me the way in which this particular clash played out at her school. Modern-style mothers who stayed home did many things for the school, serving as teacher's aides, as "home" mothers to be called in case of illness or accident, and as the chauffeurs on class outings. They envied the postmodern mothers working in Manhattan, who they imagined were living glamorous lives, eating lunch at expensive restaurants, and so on. The working mothers, in contrast, envied the stay-at-home moms, who did not have to spend long hours commuting each day or deal with the multiple stresses experienced by working women on the job.

A conflict arose whenever there was a PTA meeting. The mothers who had stayed home all day wanted an evening out and arranged for babysitters to be with the children. Working mothers, on the other hand, wanted to be with the children whom they had not seen all day and so took them to the meeting. Stay-at-home moms objected to the children being there, and working moms resented these objections. The principal tried to mediate by talking a little about the realities of both scripts, so that mothers on both sides of the issue could recognize that there were negatives as well as positives resulting from both ways of life.

She helped them shift the issue to different — not good or bad — choices.

Conclusion

Childhood socialization during the modern era was largely viewed as acquiring the new role of a student. It ignored the differences among students and among the situations in which students find themselves. By broadening our conception of childhood socialization to include frames and scripts, we can gain a better understanding of today's postmodern children and provide instruction and classroom management more effectively.

Even with this understanding, the diversity of cultures and family scripts within our postmodern society creates very difficult situations for teachers and their students. While clashes resulting from different frames and scripts usually occur just between students — or between a teacher and student —these clashes may reflect profound conflicts between quite disparate orientations and values held by families and cultures. It is therefore impossible to deal with these sorts of classroom issues without involving parents in one way or another. And just as an understanding of frames and scripts can help us work with students, it can also help teachers and parents work with one another to achieve a successful resolution when clashes arise.

Chapter 5

Reinventing Personality

The modern concept of childhood was primarily defined by the invention of the student role and the discovery of differences between age groups. Little attention was paid to the variations among children of the same age in regard to important influences on personality, such as temperament, learning style, birth order, and gender. Due to the modern beliefs in progress, universality, and regularity, young children were assumed to progress at about the same rate and to profit from the same modes of instruction. As a result, temperament, learning style. birth order, and gender differences were recognized to some extent but not translated into differentiated parenting or teaching practices.

This is changing as we move into the postmodern era, with its emphasis on difference, particularity, and irregularity. Today, both parents and teachers are more cognizant of differences in temperament, learning style, birth order, and gender, and the importance of responding to them.

The role of these aspects of personality in our reinvention of childhood quickly becomes apparent as we review the meaning of the terms used in this chapter. For example, we generally think of *temperament* as an innate disposition that helps to determine *how* we behave — as opposed to a rational reason that helps to explain *why* we behave the way we do. Some people seem endlessly energetic, while others are mostly lethargic; some people are outgoing, while others feel shy; some people adapt easily and quickly to new situations, while others become overwhelmed by demands for adaptation. These are temperamental differences that clearly influence the way young children perform and behave in the classroom, as well as in the home and in other situations.

Learning styles, on the other hand, are more specific in that they help to determine how we learn best. Some people learn best by listening, others by talking; some need absolute silence to concentrate, others require background music or noise. The resulting accomplishments and levels of proficiency may be the same, but the way in which they are achieved may be quite dissimilar. Teachers and parents who are attuned to children's learning styles can therefore help them learn more effectively, while those who are not so attuned may inadvertently squander opportunities and frustrate the children in their care.

Birth order differences are less predictable than differences in temperament and learning styles, because the effects of birth order vary with the sex of the siblings and with the age separation between them. Nonetheless, there are commonalities associated with birth order that have important parenting and instructional implications.

Likewise, *gender* differences are also important but variable, because they depend in part on individuals' psychology and on the way in which men and women are valued within a society. During the modern era, for example, a finding of differences between the sexes was often linked to a valuation of good and bad or superior and inferior — usually in favor of the male. Today, however, our postmodern perspective can help us identify, evaluate, and respond to gender differences from a less biased perspective.

Temperament

Temperament, the aspect of our personality that helps to determine how we behave, can be viewed in a number of different ways. Historically, investigators have defined it in terms of body type, social orientation, and — more recently — overall adaptability.

Temperament Based on Body Type

One modern description of adult temperament was introduced by William Sheldon, who related temperament to the predominance of one or another type of body tissue.[1] Those individuals in whom external body tissue predominates were labelled *endomorphs* by Sheldon. Such persons are generally depicted as heavyset, outgoing, and jolly. Those individuals whose body tissue is primarily of the internal type — whom Sheldon called *ectomorphs* — are usually described as thin, intellectual, socially inhibited, and introspective. A third type, whose body tissue is predominantly muscular, Sheldon called *mesomorphs*. As a group, mesomorphs were viewed as being athletic, outgoing and active.

While the connection between body tissue and temperament has not withstood close examination, Sheldon's descriptions are in keeping with stereotypical patterns that have been perpetuated in our folklore and in our literature (e.g., Friar Tuck is an endomorph, while Robin Hood is a mesomorph). Still, the problem is that many fat people are not jolly, many thin people are not intellectual, and many muscular people are not athletic. There is only a modest correlation between body type and temperament, and there is a question as to whether the body type determines the temperament or vice versa.

The Sheldon typology can nonetheless be useful, if the types are taken as general descriptions and if children are unwittingly living up to the stereotypical expectations. Mesomorphic children, for example, tend to be active and may need more physical activity than either endomorphs or ectomorphs. With endomorphs, we need to recognize that the heavy child's efforts to be funny — or his or her tendency to be assertive — are really efforts to win acceptance. The ectomorph's seclusiveness often

89

presents adults with the problem of respecting the child's rich inner world, while encouraging the child to participate in the real world as well. One strategy is to engage this sort of child in a social activity that is intellectually challenging or stimulating. Board games and games with cards often appeal to ectomorphic children.

Temperament Based on Social Orientation

The analytical psychiatrist Carl Jung introduced a different temperament typology based upon an individual's responsiveness in social situations.[2] Jung suggested that some people are *introverted* and tend to live more in their own inner world than in the real world of ongoing social encounters. When they do engage in social interactions, they tend to be shy, quiet and inhibited. Other individuals, in contrast, seem *extroverted* and are most happy when socializing. Extroverts tend to be outgoing, friendly, and talkative, abhorring a social vacuum and willing to speak to strangers on airplanes, in restaurants, and in stores. Again, these descriptions fit some people better than others, and many people are extroverted in some situations but introverted in others.

Even so, we can already see the extremes of these two temperament types during early childhood. Some children make a grand entrance into the classroom, exuding charm and personality. They totally dominate the social scene. Other children enter the classroom quietly, almost trying not to be seen or noticed. These children hold back, seldom speak up on their own, and abhor the limelight as much as the scene stealer loves it. While it is hard not to fall under the spell of the little performer, we have to make the effort and spend as much or more time with the introverted child. Perhaps the most important help we can provide for the retiring child is to find that child a friend who is responsive but not overwhelming.

90

Temperament Based on Adaptation Type

The postmodern interest in temperament variations among infants and young children is exemplified and supported by the work of psychiatrists Thomas and Chess.[3] These investigators observed and followed a large group of infants during the first year of life and at periodic intervals thereafter.

They found that some babies — the majority — generally are happy, affectionate, and responsive, eating well and sleeping regularly. These infants could be said to adapt easily and quickly to life outside the womb, and Thomas and Chess described them as *Easy to Please.*

Thomas and Chess also identified a smaller group of infants who have more trouble adapting to life outside the womb. These children tend to be cranky, wake up often during the night, and have trouble getting back to sleep. They may be irregular eaters who are at times voracious and at other times disinterested in nourishment. Eventually, however, these children adapt to the routines, eat regularly, and are emotionally responsive. Thomas and Chess called such children *Slow to Warm Up.*

A last group of children, fortunately the smallest in number, continue to have sleeping and eating problems, are chronically unhappy, and do not relate easily to their parents. These infants Thomas and Chess called *Difficult to Please.*

Thomas and Chess followed these children through the early childhood years and found that the patterns persisted well beyond infancy. These researchers did not attempt to explain the origins of these temperamental differences as either genetic or psychological, but rather assumed that they are some combination of both. Still, these temperament types seem to be the most substantial of those that have been proposed, inasmuch as they are based upon close observations of infants and follow-up studies of the same children.

Moreover, the Thomas and Chess descriptions of different adaptation types can be very useful for parents and teachers who understand that children do best when there is "goodness of fit" between the child's temperament and environmental demands. For example, a child who is slow to warm up or difficult to please may need more time in switching frames than a child who is easy to please. And because easy-to-please children are less demanding, we may tend to neglect them compared to the more demanding temperament types. It is important to remember this and give easy-to-please youngsters the attention they also need and deserve.

In ways such as this, an understanding of children's temperamental tendencies can help us anticipate and prepare for situations that may prove difficult or frustrating for young people with adaptation difficulties. When considering these temperament types, however, we need to remember that they are still broad generalizations and never fit any particular child exactly. In addition, temperament can be strongly influenced by cultural factors, and an understanding of the ways in which temperament varies in different societies is also important.

Culture and Temperament

From a postmodern perspective, we can now appreciate that non-Western cultures are not intrinsically inferior to our own —they are different and may well have things to teach us. In most Asian cultures, for example, there is a strong collective orientation that places the welfare of the group above the interests of the individual. More specifically, in the Javanese culture there is the concept of *rukun*, or peaceful harmony. From an early age, children learn to avoid conflict and to maintain this sense of tranquil non-confrontation. Rukun has a very powerful impact on temperament and is reflected in such behaviors as older children looking after younger siblings and an almost total absence of sibling rivalry. These cultural values can have a powerful influence on the temperament of all the members of a culture, as when children growing up in a society where rukun is

the guiding value continually avoid actions that might be pro-
vocative.

Other temperamental variations can also be found in Asian
cultures. Japanese children learn from an early age to distinguish between *omote*, the outer public self, and *ura*, the inner
private self. Much of the language and ritual Japanese children
learn is — at least in part — intended to help them distinguish
between the formal and informal dimensions of life. In Japanese
preschools, for example, children practice formal language,
such as "honorable mother" and "honorable father," which they
do not use every day with their parents but do use on formal occasions. Young children are also encouraged to break rules in
certain ways, such as by playing in mud, to further the distinction between the formal and the informal.

An understanding of the difference between omote and ura
is needed to fully appreciate the behavior of Japanese children in
our schools. The emphasis upon the outer, formal, standardized
self is apparent in Japanese classrooms, where conformity is the
rule and children are taught that *the nail that sticks up gets ham-
mered down*. In other words, Japanese children do not try to put
themselves ahead of their peers and appear more regimented in
the school setting than they really are. One can only fully appreciate children's individual differences in private settings, where
the ura can come to the fore.

In French-speaking cultures, temperament is affected by a
rather strict code of politeness and manners. For example, when
entering a restaurant or store in a French-speaking country, one
routinely and politely greets whoever is there with "Good morning" or "Good afternoon" or "Good evening." Likewise, when
leaving the store or restaurant, one routinely says good-bye to
everyone. From an early age, children learn these patterns of politeness with respect both to their elders and to one another, and
as a result a child's spontaneous temperamental inclinations
may be somewhat masked.

In American society, perhaps our most culturally determined temperamental characteristic — which can be seen in our children — is our hurriedness. More than 150 years ago, de Tocqueville was already commenting about this trait:

> "He who has set his heart exclusively upon the pursuit of worldly welfare is always in a hurry, for he has only a limited time at his disposal to reach, to grasp and to enjoy it. Besides the good things he possesses, he every instant fancies a thousand that death will prevent him from trying, if he does not try them soon. This thought fills him with anxiety, fear and regret and keeps his mind in ceaseless trepidation, which leads him to perpetually change his plans and his abode."[4]

Even young American children acquire this sense of urgency and feel the need to get things done quickly, so as to move on to something else. For example, American children tend to eat quickly and rush through many other activities as well. Clearly, this pattern of behavior is learned from parents, who themselves feel pressed for time and are frequently hurrying.

These cultural patterns of temperament are evident in classes where children raised in different cultures are brought together. Japanese children are usually very respectful of teachers and may feel uncomfortable calling an early childhood educator by his or her first name. (An option in this sort of situation is to use a title followed by the first name, such as "Miss Edith" or "Mr. Robert.") And French-speaking children will feel more at home if they are acknowledged in a formal way ("Good morning, Remy,") when they enter and leave the classroom. Of course, it would be best if all the children in a class addressed the teacher and were greeted in the same way. The formal greeting is actually a good idea in any case, because it gives each child verbal recognition. In this way, adapting to cultural expressions of temperament can enrich the classroom experience for all the students.

94

With respect to our American children, it is important to try to slow them down. Parents need to appreciate — and allow time for — young children's need to dawdle, to explore, and, as noted earlier, to switch frames. Setting aside time for a leisurely meal with the television off can be a particularly important way to slow things down a bit. At school, having some flexibility in the schedule and giving children an opportunity to finish projects, even though it may extend the time for that activity, can help children slow down and avoid rushing to meet the demands of an arbitrary time frame. Throughout the school day and especially on field trips, young children need to take time to observe slowly and with all of the senses.

Learning Styles

The identification of learning styles is a good example of the postmodern recognition of differences among young children. During the modern era, social scientists assumed that learning was a universal process and that the basic principles of learning held not only for all humans but for animal species as well. Today, however, we appreciate that learning differs not only between species but even among individuals of the same age and species.

Some learning styles are neurologically rooted and reflect individual preferences for sensory avenues. Other learning styles mirror individual differences in personality and temperament. Finally, as we noted in the discussion of frames, some learning styles are socially or culturally determined. We can look first at the sensory learning styles before we review those which are more socially and culturally based. An understanding of and responsiveness to these different types of learning styles is proving to be a very valuable part of our reinvention of childhood — especially at school, but also at home.

Sensory Learning Styles

Some children learn best from hearing things, others learn best from seeing things, still others learn best if they can actively explore the materials to be learned, while yet another group learns best from some combination of these modes. This does not imply, of course, that an auditory learner cannot learn visually or a visual learner cannot learn by listening — they can. But each learner has a preferred mode and will find learning easier if the material is offered primarily in this preferred mode. Knowing this, most early childhood environments now provide a mix of visual, auditory, and tactile materials to support the full range of learners in a classroom.

There are many ways of discovering a child's sensory learning style. When a storybook is shared with children, for example, those who are visually oriented will be more focused on the pictures in the book, whereas those who are more auditory will concentrate more on the words. Those children who learn best through touch often show this through their need to feel and hold the book, as well as look at it.

Similar observations can be made when children are engaged in other activities. Those who need auditory stimulation, for example, may talk to themselves while painting or working with clay. As much as possible, well-designed classroom activities should provide children with a number of different sensory avenues, so that regardless of each child's particular learning style, he or she has some comfortable path of entry into the activity.

Other sensory learning styles have to do with different children's response to distractions. One child, whose parents fixed up her room as a quiet study center complete with desk and computer, found that she was constantly coming downstairs to do her homework. She worked best amid the hubbub of family life and could not concentrate when alone in her room. Some children may need background stimulation, like music, to do their best, while others need almost complete silence. There are also children who may need to chew on an eraser or suck on hard candy to help them concentrate. Often, the need for these types of stimulation declines as the child matures, but some may persist as life-long patterns. Different environments and support systems can therefore encourage some children's learning while proving detrimental to others.

Computers can now help us individualize instruction in ways that further different learning styles. By turning written text into spoken language, for example, computers can help those young people who learn better from auditory presentations, enabling them to hear — as well as read — the material they are to learn. Likewise, the touching of the keyboard can be beneficial to those children who need tactile stimulation to learn best. It is important to remember, however, that computers primarily present written or graphic symbols, and young children need "concrete" experiences before they can begin to learn effectively through the manipulation of symbols. During early childhood, computers should play a small but still important part in helping to meet the educational needs of different children.

Personality-Linked Learning Styles

Impulsive/Reflective

Some children focus upon the goals to be achieved, and others are much more concerned with the means. In practical terms, this often translates into different patterns of exploration, experimentation, and problem solving. The goal-oriented child, for example, is inclined to do things without following or reading instructions. As a result, he or she tends to make a lot of mistakes and may need to do things over again many times. Psychologist Jerome Kagan called children with this learning style *impulsive*.[5] On the positive side, impulsive children like to learn on their own and often profit from their own mistakes, as they tend to be creative problem solvers. It is almost as if they get themselves into problem situations to force themselves to find a way out.

Other children are much more cautious when approaching a task, and Kagan called these children *reflective*. They follow directions meticulously and try to prepare carefully for all possible contingencies. They therefore like to make plans and tend to be neat and organized, with the colors of their pencil boxes matching the colors of their backpacks, and so on. Because they do not like clutter, they may even clean up after other children. However, they may also be lacking in spontaneity and creativity.

The impulsive/reflective learning styles become most significant when children are taking tests. The impulsive child is much more likely to make mistakes because of not following instructions or not reading the questions carefully. The reflective child, in contrast, has difficulties of another kind. Such children read the instructions carefully but may read too much into them and overly complicate the task. In subjects where accuracy is very important, such as math, the impulsive child will often make errors out of haste, or from not reading or following instructions. The reflective child is more likely to make mistakes because of misreading the instructions.

It may well be that culture and technology are having an impact on the impulsive/reflective learning styles. Many young children who spend a great deal of time watching television become very visually oriented and have short attention spans. These characteristics easily translate into an impulsive learning style. Parents can help minimize this effect by limiting the television watching time of their young children to no more than a couple of hours per day. At school, teachers can counteract the impact of television by engaging children in hands-on activities that really interest them and that keep them involved over longer periods of time.

Passive/Active

Passivity and assertiveness form the basis of a somewhat different pair of personality-linked learning styles. From an early age, some children are relatively passive and obedient, never challenging the authority or statements of the teacher, even when they believe something the teacher did or said was wrong. Other children are much more assertive and eager to initiate activities and question the teacher. Put differently, some children quietly accept the teacher's authority, while others do not and may actively challenge or confront the teacher.

This passive/assertive learning style difference is amplified in different cultures. As mentioned earlier, in many Asian cultures the group takes precedence over the individual. In these societies, passivity is the cultural norm, and children would not dare to challenge the teacher, who represents the school as a whole. This is true for many Native American cultures as well. For example, Native American children are reluctant to raise their hands in the classroom, because this means they are being forward and assertive.

In our "Anglo" culture, however, we encourage children to be active and to challenge us, and we become concerned about those children who are too passive and who never ask questions or challenge authority. In some cultures, this would be the norm, but in our culture it is sometimes considered virtually pathological. Likewise, societal expectations based on gender — especially regarding the assertiveness of boys and the restraint of girls — can also have a strong influence on these types of learning styles.

Lumpers and Splitters

Another learning style dichotomy that has been identified by various investigators, including Darwin, describes how different individuals approach problems of adaptation. Darwin described some people as *lumpers*, meaning that these individuals approach issues from a broad perspective, often paying little at-

99

tention to detail. Other individuals approach problems with a detailed, analytic orientation, and Darwin called these individuals *splitters*. To use a familiar analogy, splitters are people who don't see the forest for the trees, whereas lumpers are people who don't see the trees for the forest.

Society needs both lumpers and splitters. Lumpers tend to see the big picture, have substantial long-term goals, and think beyond the here and now. However, they may have difficulty moving toward their goals in a concrete way. That is where the splitters make their contribution. They may not have the big picture, but they can do the small, detailed jobs that need to get done if the big picture is ever to be realized. Statesmen tend to be lumpers, whereas accountants tend to be splitters.

Levelers and Sharpeners

Other investigators who are concerned with memory differences have re-labeled lumping and splitting as *leveling* and *sharpening*, when these orientations influence people's recollections. For example, having read a passage from a book, levelers and sharpeners tend to recall the same words in different ways. If the passage read, "On a dark, stormy April night, the creature climbed up on the shore with black-green sludge oozing out of its mouth," a leveler might recall this sentence as "On a dark night, a creature climbed up on the shore." A sharpener, in contrast, might remember "On a dark night filled with thunder and lightening, a monster crawled out of the ocean with foul-smelling black and green sludge dribbling out of its mouth."

Unlike a videotape, we do not simply record and retain exactly what has occurred. So, especially when children are being tested about what they remember, educators need to keep in mind that memories may vary for reasons beyond the children's control.

100

Birth-Order Differences

Birth-order differences reflect differences in parenting experience, as well as varying patterns in sibling interactions. This complex combination of influences results in standard types of differences, but also some variations on the birth-order theme.

First Born Children

Parents of first born children are usually young and inexperienced. Not having been around young children for quite some time, they tend to have high expectations for achievement and low levels of patience. Growing up under these circumstances, first-borns tend to be high achievers but also somewhat anxious and driven. These characteristics appear to hold true whether the first-born is a boy or a girl, and they can lead to exceptional accomplishments. A majority of the men and women who attain advanced degrees in science, medicine, and law are first-borns, as are a majority of astronauts.

When siblings come along, the oldest child is often expected to play a protective, nurturing role, and many older brothers and sisters do indeed assume this role, particularly when they are older. Although they may fight with younger siblings, a first-born child will usually stand up for the younger brother or sister if he or she is threatened by other children. Likewise, there are many stories of older brothers or sisters who have sacrificed their own education in order to help send a younger brother or sister to college.

Middle Children

The middle child is becoming an increasing rarity in today's society, where a family's size is often limited to only one or two children. Nonetheless, more than a few families still have three, four, or more children, and this can put the middle children in a difficult position, both conceptually and emotionally.

From a conceptual standpoint, middle children are neither the youngest nor the oldest and thus have a more difficult time defining their role. Should they play protector of the younger siblings or protectee of their older siblings? Should they demand the prerogatives of the older child or rail against younger children being given the same privileges they enjoy? While the oldest and the youngest have clearly defined roles, middle children must constantly vacillate between playing older and playing younger.

Middle children are also at a disadvantage emotionally and psychologically. While the oldest child had the parents all to himself or herself for a while, the middle child never has this favored position. Nor does he or she have the status of the youngest child, who is never replaced by a still younger sib and thus never has attention diverted from concerns for his or her well-being. Emotionally, middle children often feel deprived and cheated of the parental affection and attention that they believe (rightly or wrongly) is being lavished on other siblings. Not surprisingly, middle children tend to have lower career aspirations and to achieve less than either first-borns or last-borns.

Last Born Children

In some respects, last born children have the best of both worlds. On the one hand, they have a clearly defined place in the family constellation as the "baby of the family." As such, they are never replaced in their parent's affections by still another child. In addition, they have the care and the protection of older sibs, who may find them annoying but may also dote on them, as well. Last-borns tend to be outgoing and achievement-oriented, but without being as driven and anxious as the first-born. They also tend to be the most emotionally stable and caring of all the siblings, but they can be manipulative.

Only Children

Only children often share a combination of the traits of first - born and last born children. Like first-borns, whose parents were inexperienced and had high expectations, they tend to be achievement-oriented and competitive. On the other hand, like the youngest child, they have never been displaced by a younger sibling, so they have always had all the parental attention and tend to feel more secure and less anxious than first-borns. Perhaps because only children have experienced both high expectations along with exceptional attention and acceptance, they can sometimes be overbearing in the sense that they may expect everyone to treat them the same way their parents did —as special.

Variations in Birth-Order Differences

It is important to remember that the depictions of birth order patterns are generalizations to which not every first, middle, youngest, or only child conforms. For one thing, the age separation between the siblings makes an important difference. As a rule, the wider the separation, the less these stereotypic descriptions hold for the children. If, for example, the oldest child is ten or more years older than the next born, he or she is likely to act more like a parent than an older sib. In this sort of situation, the next oldest may play the role of the oldest if another sibling follows soon thereafter.

The sex of the siblings also makes a difference. Effects will differ if the sibs are all the same sex or if a brother is sandwiched in between two sisters — or vice versa. When the gender variations are combined with the matter of age separation, generalizations become more difficult to make, but what can be said is that the patterns described above hold most true when the siblings are all of the same sex and there is only a few years age separation between them.

Blended-Family Birth-Order Reversals

In our postmodern world, a new variation on the birth-order effect has resulted from the increase in blended families —couples who create a new family that includes children from an earlier marriage. These permeable families face difficulties of many kinds, particularly in the matter of loyalty (If the child becomes attached to the step-parent, is he or she being disloyal to the biological parent?) and abrupt changes in birth-order expectations.

Consider a family in which a boy is the oldest until the parent marries a spouse who has a daughter even older than the boy. The first born boy loses his special place and now has to contend with an older sister who may be inclined to boss him around. Or consider a last born child whose parent marries a spouse with an even younger child. In addition, re-married couples often have a child of their own, who not only displaces the last-born but has the special virtue of being the biological child of both parents.

Blended families can thus distort and modify the usual pattern of birth-order effects. In general, the older the children, the more difficult it will be for them to shift roles and see themselves in new birth-order positions. Yet many young people in blended families also continue to think of themselves as being in their original birth-order position and behave as if they were. This can be a cause of continual conflict if the children are not eventually willing to make accommodations to their new family arrangement.

Even with all the possible variations, an understanding of birth-order effects can be useful for the classroom teacher. In general, first-borns are best able to work on their own and take on responsibility for their own learning. Middle children often need a lot more attention and guidance, but usually do very well when this is provided. Last-borns can also work independently but are more likely to need constant approval than first-borns.

When pairing children to work together, first- and last-borns tend to work better together than either two last-borns and or two first-borns. Likewise, it is best to pair middle children with oldest children, rather than with younger or other middle children, because middle children are most in need of attention and are most likely to get it from children who were first-borns. Of course, there are always exceptions, as when some middle children do, in fact, work well together.

In the postmodern era, birth order effects have intensified in the classroom, due to the preponderance of smaller, permeable families. The relative proportion of first-borns and last-borns in any given class of children has tended to increase, while the number of middle children has declined. This means that the percentage of children in the classroom who are competitive high achievers has grown, as has the number of achievement-oriented but somewhat less competitive children. With this new mix of students, the classroom climate itself is changed, and the emphasis on achievement and competition can become quite keen. One reflection of this is that cliques — once primarily formed by young adolescents — are now appearing at ever younger age levels. Competition to get into cliques is intense, because selection is tantamount to a badge of achievement and superiority.

Gender Differences

Concern about gender differences is largely a postmodern issue. To be sure, in the modern era women fought for and won the vote, but that did not win them equal attention from social scientists, just as it did not win them equal opportunity in education and in the workplace. These issues were among the many raised by the women's movement during recent decades as part of the struggle to obtain more equal treatment.

Our postmodern reinvention of childhood has therefore included a re-examination of many gender differences. Not only were women less likely to be included in studies during the modern era, but even when they were, findings of differences were often associated with perceptions of inferiority and lesser status. In regard to math skills, for example, boys were once thought to be superior, but it has now been shown that these abilities follow a normal curve among members of each sex, so that there is much overlapping. Moreover, we now recognize that differences apparent at one age level may no longer be so at another age level, whereas others may only emerge at a later time, such as during adolescence. In any ability domain, we now recognize that the variability is such that there will always be many girls who do better than many boys.[6]

A good example of a gender difference once interpreted from a modern inferiority/superiority perspective has to do with moral development. Lawrence Kohlberg defined six stages of moral development and found that many more boys than girls attained the sixth stage of moral judgment.[7] This was interpreted to mean that girls did not attain the same level of morality as boys and might therefore be considered less moral. However, Carol Gilligan and her colleagues interpreted these findings in quite a different way.[8] They argued that girls value human relationships more than they do abstract principles, and this does not signify a lower level of moral thinking but rather a different and equally — or even more — humane morality.

This new perspective on gender differences — as real, but not indices of inferiority or superiority — has made it easier to discuss and respond to important differences without charges of sexism. Among young children, parents and educators routinely observe gender differences, and while these are often heavily socialized, they are also common enough to indicate some basic tendencies as well.

Perhaps the most obvious boy/girl difference has to do with aggressiveness, as boys tend to be more aggressive than girls. Boys fight more, play more aggressive games (i.e., war, cops and robbers), and are more resistant to authority. Girls, on the other hand, fight less, play less aggressive games (house, school), and are more respectful of authority.

106

Boys are also more muscular than girls, while girls usually have better fine-motor coordination. In addition, girls tend to have better oral language skills than boys, to read earlier, and to have fewer reading problems. Boys, meanwhile, tend to have better spatial abilities and better sensory/motor coordination (which helps them do better at video games). By school age, boys tend to like action stories while girls prefer stories about the vicissitudes of interpersonal relationships. And in the social domain, young girls appear to display more empathy with other children, as girls will provide support to a greater extent when another child is crying or unhappy.

As long as we do not attach values to these differences, recognizing that they are generalizations, and we acknowledge there are aggressive girls and passive boys, an understanding of these differences can be useful in the classroom. For example, boys tend to engage in aggressive play, and in some ways this is "the nature of the beast." It makes little sense to try to prevent such play, inasmuch as it is a natural tendency that will continue to appear. The best strategy is to allow such play but not encourage it by providing aggressive toys, such as guns. If boys want to play aggressive games with guns, let them make their own out of whatever materials are available. This will foster creativity and communicate that while we allow pretend violence, we do not condone or provide materials for such play.

The issue of gender differences grows more complex when cultural values are also involved. Even at the early childhood level, for example, boys and girls already know what toys, clothing and games are appropriate for their gender. And they are aware that it is more acceptable for a girl to be a tomboy than it is for a boy to act like a girl. Sex typing is so prevalent in the society as a whole — and in the media in particular — that it would be strange indeed if young children were not acquiring this sense of gender identity and related values.

Still, preschool children do not have the same gender biases they will acquire later and are usually happy to play with either

107

boys or girls. At this age, if children choose to play with children of the same sex, it is more a matter of preferring similar activities than it is an active rejection of the opposite sex. Indeed, pre-school children often engage in dramatic play involving both sexes, such as playing house or school. And many young children say that a child of the opposite sex is their "best friend."

One of the questions that often comes up in dealing with sex differences in early childhood settings is the extent to which across-gender play and activities should be encouraged. At the height of the women's movement, there was a great emphasis upon facilitating such play, and girls were encouraged to play with blocks and trucks, while boys were prompted to play with dolls. Much of the fervor for fostering such cross-sex play has diminished, as we appreciate that boy/girl differences are not indices of either superiority or inferiority but simply of difference. The danger, of course, is that we can then fall back upon stereotypic and evaluative thinking with regard to these differences.

This raises a difficult and fundamental issue, which applies not just to gender differences but to all the types of diversity discussed in this book. How do we help children to value and appreciate differences and not rush to judge them as bad/good and/or superior/inferior? The problem is particularly daunting in early childhood, when young children are just learning about the world and tend to regard what is familiar and comfortable as good, while also regarding all that is strange and uncomfortable as bad. We see this in particular during the second year of life, with the appearance of "stranger anxiety," which can lead a child to regard a new person with fear and trembling, even though the person may indeed be harmless. While this subsides over time, throughout the early years a child's emotions are closely tied to his or her determination of difference.

To help young children move past this stage, we need to appreciate, first of all, that it is strangeness *per se* — and not the qualities of the person or object — that is frightening to young children. We need to make every effort, then, to make the unfamiliar familiar to them. In general, this is best done gradually, rather than all at once. For example, it works better to introduce the holidays celebrated by different religious groups one at a time, rather than all at once, because young children can deal with one new thing much more easily than with a collection of new things. That is also why, in an earlier section, I suggested that an accommodation to a convention from another culture, such as a formal greeting, be extended to all children. Instead of making this greeting a matter of difference and strangeness, it can be made into something familiar and comfortable to all.

While this is more difficult to accomplish with gender differences, there are certainly things we can do to facilitate the process. Perhaps the most important is to focus on individual interests and preferences, and remain alert for any tendency —which may be unconscious or automatic — to reinforce traditional sex-role stereotypes. We should not discourage the girl who wants to play boy games, nor the boy who prefers to play with girls. Although this may be difficult at times, we best teach children the acceptance of difference by our own behavior, because in the end, it is we who are the most important indicator to children that the unfamiliar and different are not necessarily bad or something to be avoided.

Conclusion

Our postmodern recognition of the differences among same-age children now includes an appreciation of the differences in children's temperament, learning style, birth order, and gender. While there has always been at least some awareness of these differences, it is only in the postmodern era that we have begun to emphasize the importance of accepting and responding to them. Adapting parenting and educational practices to this wide range of differences complicates our role as parents and teachers, but also makes us more effective and helps to prepare children for life in our diverse society.

Chapter 6

Reinventing Intelligence and Giftedness

We generally use the term *intelligence* to mean an individual's overall ability to learn and to adapt to new situations, while the term *gifted* most often refers to those individuals who have this ability to an exceptional degree — or who demonstrate extraordinary talent in the arts, sciences, or athletics. Intelligence and giftedness were among the few traits that social scientists of the modern age recognized as varying among children at the same age level. Yet modern writers regarded intelligence as a general trait — operative in virtually all areas of behavior — while giftedness was often linked to emotional disturbance.

In the postmodern era, we have come to see intelligence as a cluster of different abilities rather than one pervasive trait, and giftedness as an indicator of superior adaptation as well as innate talent. To better understand the implications of these changes and distinctions for young children, in this chapter we will review the modern and postmodern conceptions of intelligence and giftedness, paying particular attention to the way they have been and continue to be assessed.

Intelligence in the Modern Era

The interest in measuring different people's intellectual ability was a modern phenomenon that grew out of the Enlightenment and new, humanitarian attitudes towards the insane and the retarded. Previously, the mentally ill and the mentally limited were thought to be suffering medical disorders that had to be treated in the same ways as other physical illnesses. Late in the modern era, however, these syndromes came to be understood as psychological — rather than medical — conditions. Right around the start of the twentieth century, Freud demonstrated the psychological nature of the neurosis, while Alfred Binet argued for the psychological nature of retardation and became the creator of the first modern measure of intellectual ability.

Binet (1857-1911) was trained as a lawyer but later gave up this profession, due to his growing interest in individuals' intellectual ability. He carried out and published a systematic investigation of his own two daughters and was impressed by both the similarities and differences in their performance on a variety of reasoning tasks.[1] Coincidentally, in 1904 the French minister of education announced his intention to identify children who were mentally retarded and to place them in separate schools. Binet volunteered to create a device that could be used to identify children who had limited mental abilities, but from the outset he insisted that the techniques must be psychological, and he pointed out the many problems with using only medical diagnoses of retardation. Together with his colleague Theodore Simon, Binet developed a systematic way of measuring mental ability.

In contrast to earlier researchers such as Galton, who had focused upon individual differences in reaction time and other sensory motor skills, Binet and Simon were most interested in the child's ability to reason and make sound judgments. They also wanted to measure the way these higher-order thinking processes changed with age. After experimenting with items suggested by teachers, Binet and Simon published their first scale in 1905, and they continued to refine it with a revision in 1908 and a final version in 1911, shortly before Binet's untimely death.[2]

The instrument that Binet and Simon created was an age scale in that its main purpose was to determine a child's level of intellectual development at a particular age. An item, for example, was included at the four-year-old level if 75% of a normative sample of four-year-old children could do it. If, say, 90% of four-year-olds succeeded with the item, it was too easy, and if only 15% succeeded, it was too difficult. The Binet was also an age scale inasmuch as Binet gave children an age-based score, rather than a numerical one. This score was called the child's *Mental Age*, in contrast to his or her *chronological age.*

To arrive at a child's Mental Age, Binet and Simon assigned six items to each age level, and the child was credited with two months for every item he or she passed. Thus, if a child aged four-years-and-two-months passed all the items up to the four-year level, he or she would be credited with all the months up to that age, a total of forty-eight months. If, in addition, the child also passed three of the items at the five-year level and one item at the six-year level, the child would receive an additional six months plus two months, for a total age score of fifty-six months. This total Mental Age of four years and eight months was therefore six months higher than his or her chronological age.

Binet firmly believed that intelligence should be assessed qualitatively with regard to the kinds of tasks the child was capable of mastering. And he was sure that a Mental Age score conveyed all the information one needed to make meaningful educational placements. He was thus quite modern in insisting upon the value of the child's Mental Age as his or her level of intellectual development, irrespective of the child's position in regard to other children of the same age. In many respects, Piaget (1950) modeled his notion of intelligence — age group differences in reasoning ability — on Binet's conception.

In 1916, psychologist Lewis Terman, a professor at Stanford University, created an American version of the Binet-Simon test called the *Stanford-Binet.*[3] The American scale contained many new items and was standardized on an American sample. In addition, Terman also introduced a new way of scoring a child's performance that he borrowed from the German psychologist William Stern, who first described it in 1913. This new scoring scheme involved using the ratio of mental age to chronological age mulitplied by 100 as an index of relative intellectual ability.

The ratio of mental age to chronological age is, of course, the *Intelligence Quotient* or *IQ*. In the example given earlier, the child's mental age was 56 months, while his or her chronological age was 50 months, so the IQ would be 56/50 × 100, or 112. With the introduction of the IQ, Binet testing became the first attempt to redefine intelligence as an individual difference, rather than a difference between age groups. The test was an immediate success in this country, and intelligence testing soon became a fixture of American life. During World War I, for example, intelligence tests were used to screen out those individuals whose low level of mental ability made them unfit for military service.

Intelligence in the Postmodern Era

The postmodern reinvention of intelligence is, of course, a gradual and ongoing process, but the work of psychologist David Wechsler can serve as a rough marker of its beginning. In 1939, Wechsler published what is now known as a *point scale* of intelligence.[4] On the Wechsler Scales, the subject is given a point score for success or failure on particular items, rather than a score defined in years and months as on the Binet. However, using statistical tables derived from a database of a large normative sample, these numerical scores can be converted into mental ages. Additional tables that plot mental age against chronological age can then be used to arrive at the IQ for any particular mental/chronological age combination.

In addition to creating the point scale scoring of his adult, child, and preschool tests, Wechsler also introduced several other innovations that reflected the postmodern interest in particularity. First of all, he divided his intelligence tests into a *Verbal* and a *Performance* scale, each of which consisted of a number of sub-scales. These, in turn, contained items of a particular type, with the Verbal scales including such subtests as

114

vocabulary (assessing knowledge of words), information (assessing knowledge of facts), and similarities (assessing knowledge of similarities and differences). The Performance subtests include block design (assessing the ability to copy geometrical patterns), picture completion (assessing the ability to identify missing parts of familiar objects), and picture arrangement (assessing the ability to arrange pictures into a causal sequence). Unlike the Verbal tests, the Performance tests are timed.

With the Wechsler Scales, therefore, we can obtain a Verbal score and a Performance score, as well as a General intelligence score. In addition, by plotting a subject's performance on the various subtests the examiner can obtain an individual *profile* of performance that provides a graphic portrait of the particular individual's intellectual strengths and weaknesses. In this way, Wechsler's scales move intelligence testing into the postmodern era, as they illustrate the wide differences in patterns of mental ability among children of the same age level.

These patterns — or profiles — of ability are important because two children who attain the same General IQ scores may nonetheless display quite different patterns of ability. One child, for example, who scores high on the Verbal subtests may do much more poorly on the Performance measures, while another child tops the Performance tests but falls down on the Verbal measures. So, while these two children ended up with the same General score, the way in which they attained it was quite different. Profile analysis is, therefore, a very important part of interpreting individual intelligence test results.

The original Wechsler Scales were designed to measure adult intelligence, but in 1949 Wechsler introduced a point scale of intelligence for children. Known as the WISC, it has been revised several times since then and is now known as the WISC-R.[5] And in 1967, Wechsler published a point score intelligence test for preschool and primary school children (ages 3-7), the WPPSI, which was revised in 1987 as the WPPSI-R.[6] These early childhood scales are modeled after the adult scales, with children assigned both verbal and performance scores as well as profiles of their various specific abilities.

The Wechsler Scales suggested that the concept of general intelligence, presupposed by the Binet, was too broad and needed to be broken down into smaller components. This sort of breakdown was first proposed by Charles Spearman, who argued that test intelligence consisted of a number of factors.[7] He believed a general or "g" factor was genetic in origin and was analogous to the amount of mental energy available to the individual. In addition, he proposed that there were a number of other "s" or specific factors, which represented particular abilities in areas such as mathematics, literacy, and music. The "g" factor, however, was the dynamic force behind — and set the limits for — the "s" factors. Other writers, such as Thurstone[8] and Guilford,[9] used the statistical method of factor analysis in their attempts to substantiate Spearman's theory. All these researchers thus anticipated the postmodern challenge to the concept of intelligence as a unified construct, as well as the postmodern postulation of more than one type of intelligence.

Although the modern conception of intelligence as a unified ability has not entirely been abandoned, it is nonetheless being redefined to incorporate the idea of mental power as a pattern or cluster of abilities rather than a single trait. Three contemporary advocates of a more differentiated conception of intelligence, John Horn, Robert Sternberg, and Howard Gardner, have made major contributions to this reformulation of intelligence as part of postmodern childhood.

John Horn has argued that general intelligence is of two major kinds — *fluid* and *crystallized*.[10] Some intelligence subtests measure on-the-spot reasoning and problem solving, which he termed fluid abilities. Many of the Performance tests on the WISC, such as block design, measure fluid intelligence. Crystallized intelligence, in contrast, is assessed by those subtests that tap accumulated knowledge, such as vocabulary. One interesting finding based on this perspective is that fluid intelligence declines with age more rapidly than does crystallized intelligence.

Robert Sternberg[11] has proposed what he calls a *triarchic* — or components — theory of intelligence. One set of components are those that enable the individual to plan, monitor, and evaluate problem-solving performance (metacomponents). Then, there are the processes actually involved in carrying out tasks (performance components). Finally, there are knowledge components used in acquiring, sorting, and organizing information. From this contextual perspective, intelligence is evaluated in terms of how well the individual adapts to a particular environment, rather than from the standpoint of general adaptive ability.

An even more widely disseminated postmodern approach to intelligence is that of Howard Gardner, who argues that there is not one general intelligence but rather seven particular — and largely unrelated — *multiple intelligences.*[12] According to Gardner, these seven intelligences are logical/mathematical, linguistic, musical, spatial, bodily/kinesthetic, interpersonal, and intrapersonal. While some of these are routinely regarded as intellectual abilities, others, such as the musical, have traditionally been regarded as talents. Nonetheless, these ideas have been widely adopted in early childhood education.

In short, the modern conception of intelligence as a unified ability to reason and adapt to new situations — and as an ability that varied between age groups — has largely been replaced by the concept that intelligence is a cluster of related abilities that vary among children of the same age.

Intelligence Testing and Early Childhood Education

During the modern era, intelligence testing of young children was quite limited. One reason is that there were relatively few programs for young children. In many states, kindergarten was not mandated, and nursery schools were half-day affairs considered to be an outing and social activity for mother and child, and so something of a luxury. When tests were used to evaluate children in this age group, it was primarily for diagnostic or selective purposes. That is, intelligence tests were used to identify the retarded, or to determine whether a child should be admitted to kindergarten or first grade if he or she was younger than the school system's cut-off age for entrance. For the most part, however, testing in general — and intelligence testing in particular — was relatively uncommon at the early childhood level.

All this changed after the 1960s and the momentous changes in the family and in society. Just as many mothers of young children were returning to the work force, some writers proposed that formal instruction should be used to capitalize on the rapid intellectual growth that occurs during early childhood. The idea was that young children could learn faster and better at an early age, and that early academic experiences could raise children's IQ. Unfortunately, some early childhood programs, which were growing at exponential rates at that time, did introduce formal instruction and used intelligence tests to demonstrate the efficacy of this practice. As a result, the start of the postmodern era was a time when intelligence test scores began to be linked to the achievement of young children, rather than being used just for diagnosis or selection, as was the practice during the modern era.

The belief in the early academic competence of young children also led to renewed interest in Montessori. As noted earlier in this book, Montessori had expressed confidence in young children's competence and their ability to learn the basics of reading, writing, and math. What Montessori appreciated, however, in contrast to some postmodern promoters of early childhood intelligence, was that the materials had to be developmentally appropriate. That is, a skill like reading could be introduced through the use of sensory-motor materials like sandpaper letters, as opposed to formal instruction in sound/symbol correspondence.

Other early childhood programs, including the Head Start programs that were federally legislated in 1967 to serve disadvantaged children, were also encouraged to introduce reading, math, and science. Fortunately, many different models were explored in these programs, not just the academic approach.

A number of studies have since provided more information on the efficacy of early instruction and its effect on children's IQ. Most of the studies indicated that while there were some short-term gains in IQ, these were not lasting and were probably improvements in performance rather than true gains in intellectual potential. On the other hand, important long-term benefits did result from high-quality early childhood education programs that did not rely heavily on formal instruction. The most comprehensive study of such effects was carried out by the High Scope Organization.[13] Children who had attended its early childhood programs, as well a control group of children who did not attend the programs, were followed for more than eighteen years. The researchers found that children who attended the early childhood program were far more likely to graduate from high school, to get good jobs, and *not* to have a criminal record than were comparable children who did not attend these programs. Early childhood education turned out to be important to these children not because it changed their intellectual potential, but rather because it helped them obtain the social and other readiness skills needed to succeed academically and vocationally.

With several decades of research on early childhood education behind us, we can conclude that the reinvention of early childhood as a crucial period for beginning formal instruction and raising children's IQ did not work as planned. A more appropriate and effective reinvention of early childhood education and the role of intelligence is now growing out the ideas of Wechsler, Thurstone, Guilford, Horn, Sternberg, and Gardner. By viewing intelligence as a pattern of related abilities that vary from individual to individual, early childhood educators can develop age-appropriate programs that meet the differing needs of their diverse student population.

This postmodern concept of intelligence has also given rise to new types of assessment that move away from the formal testing tradition and instead reflect the postmodern conception of intelligence as different, particular, and irregular. At the preschool level, as at later age levels, *portfolios* of the child's work — drawings, writings, constructions — allow children to demonstrate their abilities and knowledge in unique ways, which can reveal strengths that formal tests would not have shown. In a similar way, *projects* that children undertake, whether putting on a play or building a castle, also allow adults to assess children's varied capacities and ways of showing what has been learned. Finally, the child's actual *performance* —whether the recital of a poem or mental addition and subtraction — can also provide evidence of individual intellectual accomplishment. The increasing use of these assessment techniques supports and documents the postmodern reinvention of intelligence.

Giftedness in the Modern Era

A young man once asked Mozart how to go about writing a symphony. Mozart suggested that he begin with something less ambitious, like a song. The young man took umbrage at this and said to Mozart, "But you wrote a symphony at age three." To which Mozart replied, "That is true enough, but I did not have to ask how."

Giftedness — whether in general intelligence or in the arts, the sciences or athletics — has traditionally been perceived as something that you are born with and discover that you have. While it cannot be acquired with any amount of training or effort, it also is not always realized, because the individuals who are gifted may not have the motivation, temperament, or opportunity to make the efforts required for exceptional talent to reach its full potential. Giftedness is thus a necessary but not a sufficient condition for developing exceptional talent, which can also be affected by the way it is perceived within a particular society.

During the modern era, there was a widespread belief that giftedness was associated with deviance and mental illness, and that gifted or unusually precocious children would end badly. "Early ripe, early rot" was the phrase often used to epitomize this belief. In support of this prejudice, newspapers reported stories about people such as the young man who graduated Harvard at 12, M.I.T. at 15 and taught mathematics there at the age of 18. At the age of 21, however, he was living in a one-room apartment, collecting street car transfers.

It was in part to counter these modern views about giftedness, that psychologist Lewis Terman, the creator of the Stanford-Binet intelligence test mentioned earlier, undertook a longitudinal investigation of the intellectually gifted. In 1921, he received a grant from the Foundation Fund of New York to study 1,000 children who had IQ's of 140 or higher. After the children became part of the study, Terman and his colleagues monitored them for the next thirty years, testing them in 1927-1928, 1939-1940, and 1951-1955. Here are some of the findings Terman reported:

> "The incidence of mortality, ill health, insanity, and alcoholism is, in each case below that of the generality of corresponding age...the great majority are still well

121

adjusted socially and...the delinquency rate is but a fraction of what it is in the general population...As for schooling, close to 90 percent entered college and 70 percent graduated. Of those graduating, 30 percent were awarded honors and about two-thirds remained for graduate work. The educational record would have been much better but for the fact that a majority reached college age during the great depression."[14]

These studies were decisive in countering the belief that giftedness was associated with mental dysfunction. A number of other investigators undertook their own longitudinal investigations of the gifted and generally obtained results comparable to those described by Terman (Hollingsworth and Kaunitz,[15] Witty,[16] Hildreth[17]), showing that the gifted are not only higher achievers, but are also physically healthier and better adjusted than those of average ability. With respect to the gifted, therefore, nature is essentially generous rather than vindictive.

On the other hand, it is also true that Terman's intellectually gifted children had highly educated parents and came from middle- to upper-class homes. Certainly, genetic endowment played a role in the success of these gifted children, but the environment also played a role. Many children with similar potential may never fully realize their abilities, simply because they are growing up in environments that are less intellectually nourishing than those experienced by the children in many of the longitudinal studies of giftedness.

Fortunately, most parents play a positive role in helping gifted children realize their talents, and the importance of this supportive role has been demonstrated in a number of studies. In one investigation of talented individuals who attained eminence by the age of forty, parental support and encouragement — rather than pressure — was the common denominator.[18] This study found that if a child expressed an interest in drawing, for example, the parents provided the necessary tools and the time and place to use them. In the early stages, formal lessons were less important — almost contraindicated — than allowing the child to find his or her own way before learning the prescribed method. Parents were important for Terman's gifted children, but he did not focus on this as much as he did on the achievements of his subjects.

Although Terman was among the first to study the intellectually gifted in a systematic way, he was still modern in his attitudes towards other differences. For example, when he discovered that girls scored higher on Binet tests than did boys, he and his co-workers then adjusted the items of the tests, so that the two sexes scored about equally. At the same time, Terman made no provisions to correct for differences between racial and social class groups, as he and his colleagues assumed these were reflective of true intellectual differences, rather than test bias differences. In the modern era, and, unfortunately, even today, IQ test scores that may be biased against certain groups are still used as evidence that the members of such groups have less ability.

Giftedness in the Postmodern Era

The reinvention of early childhood in the postmodern era has included a recognition of the need for developmentally appropriate practice to meet the needs of gifted children. Identifying truly gifted children at the early childhood level, however, is made difficult by the apparent precocity of most children at this age level. This results from the fact that young children are wonderful mimics and have extraordinary short-term memories. A child, for example, may be able to recite the numbers from one to fifty correctly, but the same child may not be able to count even six actual objects correctly. Reciting numbers is simply an index of verbal memory and does not reflect a real ability to count. Perhaps this is why Goethe said that, "If children grew up according to early indications, we should have nothing but geniuses."

123

There are a number of ways, however, in which truly gifted and talented children demonstrate their abilities while still very young. The child may, for example, display unusual problem solving with block building, or he or she may show extraordinary originality in storytelling, in dramatic play, or in singing or playing an instrument. Many gifted children display a hunger for books even at ages 3 and 4. One mother described her 5-year-old daughter as follows:

> "She can count to 100 and beyond with no difficulty, and can write the numbers from 1 to 25. She recognizes every letter of the alphabet, can print each letter in large and small letters, and also prints about three dozen words. She has taught herself how to pick out tunes on the piano after hearing them once or twice. Her memory is remarkably keen, too."[19]

A more quantitative measure of intellectual giftedness can easily be obtained with standard intelligence tests (children who attain IQ's of 140 or more are generally regarded as "intellectually gifted"). In addition, postmodern thinkers have also devised a number of measures to assess creativity. These measures are also important because intellectual giftedness is generally regarded as superiority in *convergent* thinking, while creativity reflects superiority in *divergent* — or unconventional — thinking.[20] And children who are gifted in convergent thinking are not necessarily gifted in divergent thinking, or vice versa.[21]

One of the general measures of creativity is known as the "alternative uses" task. A subject is asked to list as many uses as he or she can imagine for a familiar object (e.g., "How many uses can you think of for a nail?"). A second measure of creativity is to present the subject with an unusual situation and ask him or her to imagine as many different consequences as possible ("The earth's surface is entirely covered with water in three months, except for the highest mountain peaks. Write as many consequences as you can.") In their research, Getzels and Jackson gave children fables with the last line missing and asked the children to complete the fable.[23] They also asked children to give as many meanings as they could to squiggly nonsense drawings. On all these measures, the children's responses are scored not only in terms of their number, but also their originality.

Using either IQ or creativity measures, identifying truly gifted children is relatively easy, even at an early age. How to best educate such children presents more challenging problems.

The Gifted and Early Childhood Education

During the early and middle decades of the twentieth century, educational programs for gifted young children consisted primarily of early admittance to kindergarten and acceleration through the grades. For example, beginning in 1932, children in Brookline, Massachusetts were admitted to kindergarten on the basis of their Mental Age as well as their chronological age. All children were admitted to kindergarten if they were four years and nine months of age on October 1st. In addition, children who were chronologically younger but who attained MA's of four years and ten months (later raised to five years) were also admitted. As a result, some children as young as four years of age were admitted to kindergarten on the basis of their MA. These early entrants ranged in IQ from 107 to 125.

A follow-up study of these children was conducted over a ten-year period.[23] In first grade and in each of the succeeding years, the younger children received more A's and B's, had fewer failures and trial promotions, and had higher test scores.

A number of studies in other states reported similar results. Of particular importance was a study of children attending rural schools in Lancaster County, Nebraska.[24] The subjects were a group of children all of whom entered school at five years of age or younger, and who were given a mental ability and achievement test during the seventh month of fourth grade. The study found that children's Mental Age was significantly more influential in determining the children's achievement than was their chronological age, their IQ, or some combination of the two.

Although these data were collected during the modern era, they have important implications for contemporary early childhood education. There is an ongoing controversy about what is the appropriate age for children's entrance into kindergarten and whether or not to hold children back who are not "ready" for first grade. What some of these policies ignore, and what the Nebraska study reflects, is that early childhood is a period of very rapid intellectual growth, and children with the same IQ's may nonetheless grow at different rates. The MA is therefore a better measure of intellectual growth rate than is the IQ, in that the MA measures the child's qualitative progress, such as his or her attainment of Piaget's concrete operations. And it is the attainment of these operations, rather than IQ or chronological age, that is the most important factor ensuring a child's success with formal instruction.

Other than early admission to kindergarten, there was little provision for gifted and talented young children in the modern period. Even the early-admission programs were limited to those states and communities that had kindergartens, and in many states kindergarten was not an educational requirement.

In the postmodern era, three general strategies have evolved for working with gifted young children. One that we have already talked about in connection with kindergarten entrance is *acceleration*. As previously noted, if children are accelerated on the basis of MA they do better than when promoted on the basis of either chronological age or IQ. Another strategy is to use *pull-out* programs in which children spend some time outside the regular classroom with a teacher who provides enrichment over and above what is offered in the regular classroom. A third strategy is to provide *special schools* for the gifted, such as the one attached to Hunter College in New York City.

Given the current emphasis on *inclusion*, many gifted children will remain in regular classrooms and be offered these sorts of programs. However, this places special demands on the early childhood educator, as teaching the gifted requires a delicate balance of challenging the gifted without making the other children feel inadequate or less self-confidant. This can be accomplished by establishing a sense of group identity in which all children in the class feel valued and a part of the whole. In general, the goals for teaching gifted and talented young children are the same as those for teaching all young children:

1. Helping them to gain a mastery of oral language, literacy, and numerical skills.

2. Helping them learn essential facts about common things.

3. Helping them gain a wide range of new concepts.

4. Helping them to think critically and to challenge.

5. Helping them to acquire good work and study skills.

6. Helping them to learn the social skills required for successful interpersonal interactions.

7. Helping them to learn how to plan and carry out a program of learning and to cooperate with others in such planning.

Working with gifted and talented children is indeed a daunting teaching assignment, but it can be richly rewarding when observing the progress such children make. If we provide appropriate stimulation while remembering that the gifted and talented are still children, and if we generate a sense of the group so that all children have a sense of belonging and contributing, the entire class will be enriched.

Of course, parents with gifted children also face special problems. For example, with these children the issue is not how to stimulate them intellectually, but rather how to keep up with them and help them modulate their voracious intellectual appetites. Gifted children sometimes become too involved with their work and do not take enough time to play and socialize with other children. Parents need to make sure that the child does take time out for friends and non-academic pursuits. In addition, while meeting the special needs of a gifted child, parents also must work hard not to treat the gifted child differently in other respects than less gifted brothers or sisters, although giftedness often runs in families and other siblings may have similar gifts.

For exceptionally gifted children, an adult mentor in the child's field of interest can be an enormous help. Many high school and college teachers are willing to work with such gifted young children. For children who are artistically — rather than intellectually — gifted, it is important not to impose formal instruction on the young child too early. Encouraging a musical child by having instruments available, or encouraging an artistic child by providing drawing materials, is really all that is needed during early childhood, as formal instruction might interfere with the child's spontaneity. The child can always learn the more formal aspects of a discipline later.

In early childhood, the most important thing is to help the young child find his or her own way, and this remains true in later years as well. When George Gershwin went to Paris to study with Debussy, Debussy asked, "Why would you want to be a second-rate Debussy when you can be a first-rate Gershwin?" True talent finds its own means of expression, which may include creating new rules rather than simply following old ones.

Conclusion

In the postmodern era, intelligence and giftedness are increasingly being recognized as multifaceted capabilities that differ according to the particular people and situations in which they are found. There is also a widespread recognition of the importance of responding to the differences among individuals in regard to intelligence and giftedness. This, in turn, puts pressure on adults to find the right balance between meeting the needs of individual children and helping them experience the sense of belonging and normalcy that comes from being part of a group. As we will see in the next chapter, this same challenge also applies to a wide range of children who are now considered to have "special needs."

Chapter 7

Reinventing Normality

The modern conception of childhood largely excluded children with special needs. During the modern era, the emphasis on universality, regularity, and progress led to an idealized perception of children, and in many cases to an inclination to ignore children whose needs made them seem different, irregular, and limited.

In this country, although children who had special needs were regarded as a group apart, there was at least some public concern and accommodation for them, especially during and after the nineteenth century. What has changed in the postmodern era is the extent to which these needs are recognized, and the way in which adults and institutions are now responding to them. This is particularly true in regard to young children, as most of the attention to special needs in the modern era was directed towards children of school age.

To fully understand this aspect of the reinvention of childhood, we first need to consider the changes in the understanding and perception of special needs that occurred during the twentieth century. And as these changes have been part of an extensive "reinvention of normality" for people of all ages, we need to view them in this context and then focus on the implications for young children.

Changing Perceptions of Special Needs

The modern perception that children and adults who had special needs were a group apart led to the creation of separate institutions to accommodate them, to the extent they were accommodated at all. In the early decades of the nineteenth century, for example, coincident with the introduction of free public schools, educational facilities for children with special needs were also established. These were, however, for children with the most readily apparent disabilities — blindness and deafness. It was assumed that children with these disabilities could not function in regular schools and in the everyday world, so separate residential schools were established for them. The Fernald School for the Blind, in Waltham, Massachusetts, was one of the first such schools and is still in operation.

Once blind and deaf children were placed in these schools, they were often ignored and forgotten by the larger society. Few efforts were made to give these children the skills they needed to survive and succeed on their own. Moreover, there were no public accommodations for people who had disabilities — no ramps, railings, or signs in Braille, for example. In these and other ways, people who had special needs were not encouraged to become an integral part of their communities.

Interestingly, it was World War II that served as a catalyst for changing attitudes towards people who had special needs. The nationwide draft of young men into the armed services, along with the improved physical and psychological screening of these men, led to some unexpected findings. It was discovered that large numbers of potential recruits had either physical or mental problems sufficient to prevent their being inducted into military service. This was often a shock, because up until the time of testing, many of these young men had lived, gone to school, and worked in their communities. To a large extent, they were considered no different than anyone else, and the discovery that so many "normal" young men had special needs led to an increased willingness to recognize and respond to these needs. This, in turn, opened up more educational and vocational opportunities than had previously been available for individuals with disabilities.

World War II also had a powerful impact on attitudes about special needs in another way, as well. As with other recent conflicts, improved medical care enabled many more men to survive despite being seriously injured or maimed. In more than a few cases, young men who had been well integrated into the community returned without limbs or in wheelchairs or with serious visual or auditory problems. The effect these men had on their communities was even stronger than that of the people who had been found to have disabilities during their initial screening. Because the wounded veterans had made exceptional sacrifices for their country, intense efforts were made to rehabilitate them and encourage them to return to as normal a family and occupational life as possible. In this way, the large number of seriously wounded veterans further hastened the reinvention of normality to include people who had disabilities.

The changing perceptions of people with disabilities soon spread to the parents of children who had special needs. Up until the end of World War II, many parents refused to acknowledge such children. Of course, this was more true for some disabilities than for others, and parents of a mentally retarded or epileptic child were often particularly reluctant to acknowledge the existence of a such a child in their home. An extreme case was a father in California, who feared his daughter was retarded and therefore kept her locked in a barren room for the first twelve years of her life.

It was not just the negative attitudes of other people that kept parents from responding to children with disabilities. Unless you have experienced in your own home the trauma of a child who has disabilities, it is hard to appreciate the emotional turmoil that can result. Many parents blamed themselves for their child's disability and were reluctant to acknowledge it out of guilt. In other families, one parent might blame the other for

133

causing the disability, as when one mother accused her husband of "getting even with her" by giving her a retarded child. Of course, many parents did accept and respond to their disabled children but could find little help or support within their communities. They then bore the enormous burden of very difficult child care without additional help.

Around the time of World War II, the growing acceptance of individuals with disabilities encouraged parents of children with handicaps to organize and work together to improve the lot of their offspring, including children whose disabilities had not been previously recognized or attended to. In 1940, the mother of a child who had cerebral palsy advertised in The New York Times, asking parents of similar children to contact her. Many parents responded, and this became the impetus for what is now the New York State Cerebral Palsy Association. Parents of children with cerebral palsy were the first to organize on a local, state, and — eventually — national level, and parents of children with other disabilities soon followed suit. For example, the National Association for Retarded Children was established a few years after the start of the cerebral palsy associations.

Parent organizations such as these soon became a powerful pressure group for national recognition of children with special needs. The organizations lobbied not only for more adequate educational facilities but also for more research into the causes of the disabilities. Largely as a result of these efforts, the U.S. government began to support extensive research projects looking into the determinants and potential treatments of cerebral palsy and other disabilities.

In addition to the research efforts, the government also funded specialized teacher and leadership training programs at many colleges and universities. "Facilities grants" for demonstration centers were awarded, as were "stimulation grants" for innovative programs. As a result, within a ten-year span more than one hundred colleges and universities had teacher training programs, research initiatives, and/or demonstration projects on site.

All these influences and activities helped to bring about the postmodern reinvention of normality, in which special needs are no longer considered a *stigma* to be hidden and denied, but rather a common and acceptable *challenge* for rehabilitation, education and research. This postmodern perspective was made official by the federal legislation known as Public Law 94-142, the Individuals with Disabilities in Education Act (IDEA), which was passed by Congress in 1975. Along with more recent amendments to it, this law requires local education authorities to:

1. Identify the special needs of students through non-discriminatory assessment.

2. Involve parents in developing each child's educational program.

3. Create a minimally restrictive environment for the child.

4. Develop an Individual Education Program (IEP) of study for each child who has a disability.

To meet these requirements, educators have tried a number of different strategies. One of the first and most widely used practices has been *mainstreaming*, which involves moving children from segregated educational facilities into regular classrooms. This enables children with special needs to interact with other children, and vice versa. However, teachers with mainstreamed children in their classes often have not received the support services they need to teach the special-needs children in their classes effectively.

Some of the difficulties with mainstreaming led educators to try a new concept known as the *least restrictive environment* (LRE). Ideally, such an environment provides special-needs children with as normal a setting as possible while still meeting their special academic, social, and physical needs. The LRE approach is much broader than mainstreaming and offers a range of possibilities from mainstreaming to placement in a special facility, depending on the needs of the child.

A third approach, called *inclusion*, places children with special needs in a regular classroom to the fullest extent possible, but also is supposed to offer a comprehensive and coordinated combination of services, which can be provided in places other than the school. Of course, this approach is dependent on the availability of appropriately trained classroom teachers and all the needed special services.

The IDEA law and the program strategies developed in response to it were aimed at elementary school children. Increasingly, however, similar strategies have been extended down to the preschool level, so today parents of young children who have special needs may be able to find the same options available to school-age children. Yet, the inclusion of special-needs children within a regular early childhood classroom poses unique problems, because a young child who has special needs is not just a smaller version of an older child with the same disabilities. A young blind or deaf child, for example, has to cope with different problems as a preschooler than he or she will face after having learned Braille or lip reading.

In addition, the active, sensory-oriented preschool environment may be particularly valuable for some special-needs children, such as those with severe visual limitations, while a more communication-oriented curriculum may be more helpful for children with limited hearing. In short, young children who have special needs require an educational emphasis appropriate to their particular capabilities and limitations as well as to their developmental level, and this may exceed what a regular preschool teacher and classroom can provide.

To determine which educational strategies can best be used to meet children's different needs, we will first review the wide range of special needs found among students today, and then consider ways to develop effective strategies that meet those needs.

Sensory Disabilities

Hearing Impairment

A relatively small proportion of special-needs children suffer from auditory impairments, which are usually divided into two levels. A child with a *partial* hearing impairment wears a hearing aid or aids and so can hear enough to function in a regular classroom. A child who is *deaf* has so little hearing that he or she needs to communicate through other sensory or motor channels — usually by using sign language and lip reading. There are many different causes of these hearing impairments, ranging from the genetic to rubella (German measles) and middle ear infections during infancy.

There remains considerable disagreement among professionals as to the best educational approach for young deaf children. One group of experts, known as the *oral* group, argues that young deaf children should *not* be taught to sign and instead should be forced to use whatever residual hearing they have in order to learn how to speak. In this way, the children avoid what is called "deaf voice" — the toneless speech of those who have learned to speak without ever hearing language. Other experts, known as the *manual* group, believe young children should learn to sign as soon as possible, so that they can begin to communicate. Today, most professionals take a middle position in favor of *total communication*, which makes the top priority giving the child whatever means of communication works best.

In our public schools, about 92 percent of deaf children are in full-time or part-time special education classes. About half of these children spend at least some time in regular classrooms, while most students with partial hearing impairment are in regular classrooms full-time. Younger children with partial hearing can also be successfully included in regular early childhood programs, but young deaf children may need to spend more time in special classes, where they can learn to sign and lip read. When young deaf children are included in a regular early childhood program, it is very beneficial if the teacher knows at least some basic sign language, which is now taught in many early childhood training programs.

Visual Impairment

Children who have severe visual disorders probably comprise the smallest group of children who have special needs. While about one of every ten children entering schools has some form of visual impairment, most of these problems can be corrected by lenses, surgery, or therapy. Only about one in a thousand children has a significant *visual disability* that cannot be corrected and may interfere with the child's learning in a regular classroom. A child who has this sort of visual disability is likely to need individual attention and training before moving into a regular classroom. But for young children who have less severe visual problems, the manipulative activities with hands-on materials emphasized in regular early childhood programs are particularly important, as they help the children obtain information through their other senses.

Communication Disorders

These disorders are generally organized into two categories, *expressive* disorders and *receptive* disorders. Children with expressive disorders have trouble forming and sequencing sounds. Some expressive disorders, such as stuttering, are chronic and require professional help outside the classroom. Other expressive disorders, such as articulation difficulties (saying *yeyo* for *yellow*), are often developmental and disappear with maturation. Articulation problems are especially common when children are young, and with such children it is important to remember that their problem is expressive rather than receptive. That is, they can hear and recognize the sound an *L* makes, for example, they just can't say it. This becomes clear when you repeat the articulation error to the child, who may respond, "Not *yeyo. Yeyo.*"

Receptive disorders include difficulties understanding language and its use to communicate ideas. Many children's receptive language problems turn out to be a symptom of other problems, such as a hearing impairment, a learning disability, or mental retardation. Receptive language problems can also resemble — but should not be confused with — difficulties caused by a disadvantaged background or one in which English is a second language. Children who have backgrounds such as these may simply need additional exposure to and instruction in our language, in order for them to increase their comprehension.

With the exception of stuttering and stammering, communication disorders are often more difficult to diagnose in young children. A young child's inability to understand, for example, may stem from inattention, lack of familiarity with the words being used, or another external factor. I therefore believe that in early childhood classrooms we should give children the benefit of the doubt and not rush to identify the child as having a communication disorder, unless it is severe enough to hinder his or her effective participation in a group. Even if the child does have a mild receptive disorder, it usually will do little harm, and the child may benefit more if he or she is accepted like the other children and not singled out.

Mental Retardation

Mental retardation has been defined by the American Association on Mental Retardation as follows:

139

"Mental retardation refers to substantial limitations in present intellectual functioning. It is characterized by significantly sub-average intellectual functioning existing concurrently with related limitations in two or more of the following applicable adaptive skill areas: communication, self-care, home living, social skills, community use, self-direction, health and safety, functional academics, leisure, and work. Mental retardation manifests itself before age 18."[1]

The designation of mental retardation is usually based on individual intelligence test scores. Although there are many classifications of retardation, the most useful for educational purposes is a three-level division that corresponds roughly with Piaget's stages of intellectual development. In considering these divisions, it is important to remember that intelligence test scores represent ranks and that the groupings are far from exact. It is also important to recall the postmodern conception of intelligence as a cluster of abilities rather than a unitary one. These ideas have not yet been widely accepted in regard to retardation, but their implications are that while the groupings are useful as general guidelines, the individual child and his or her demonstrated capacities should always be the deciding factor, not the test score.

Traditionally, children are termed *educable* if they attain an IQ score between 50 and 70. Although such children are slow, they may not be identified until they enter school. These children generally acquire Piaget's concrete operations but never attain formal operations. As a consequence, they seldom succeed academically beyond the sixth-grade level. On the other hand, many of these children can adapt quite well socially and can be mainstreamed during elementary school. As adults, they can often hold jobs that require simple skills (e.g., a packer in a supermarket) and can live independently with some supervision.

Children who attain IQ scores between 35 and 55 are termed *trainable*. These children acquire only the rudiments of Piaget's concrete operations but do attain the symbolic function. They can learn to walk and talk, although these motor and verbal skills never reach the level of proficiency attained by educable children. At best, they can reach the second-grade level in regard to academic skills, and they benefit from some training in social and very simple occupational skills. Some of these children can be included in schools at an early age, but only with considerable support services provided by specially trained teachers.

The most severely retarded children score between 0 and 20 on an IQ test and are termed *custodial*. At best, these children attain Piaget's sensory-motor level of ability and acquire object permanence. They can also learn some simple communication and hygiene skills with training. As the term "custodial" suggests, these children must receive full-time care.

Thanks to the postmodern policies of mainstreaming and inclusion, educable and trainable children tend to receive more intellectual stimulation and realize their abilities to a greater extent than they would have during the modern era. Mainstreaming and inclusion are especially beneficial during the early childhood period, when these children are less different than their peers and can acquire some sense of being the same as their age mates, as well as different from them.

Learning Disabilities

The National Joint Committee on Learning Disabilities describes these problems as "significant difficulties in acquiring and using listening, speaking, reading, writing, reasoning, or mathematical skills." The overall category of learning disabilities is a postmodern one and was first described in the early 1960s. It now is comprised of the largest group of children with special needs — about 4 percent of the school-age population. Most of these learning disabled children are of average intelligence, and their disability is often limited to a particular domain, such as reading, so it would not necessarily affect their learning in another domain, such as mathematics.

Of course, learning problems can have many causes, including genetic ones, illness, and stress. It is often the case, for example, that children with learning difficulties have parents who had similar disabilities, but it is not always clear whether this was the result of genetic transmission, modeling or parenting style.

Learning disabilities pose special problems for early childhood educators because these disorders are usually determined only after the child has begun formal instruction in tool subjects. Nonetheless, even at the preschool level, it is sometimes possible to identify children who may later have trouble learning these subjects. Preschool children who consistently have trouble listening and following instructions, who are unable to start a task and bring it to completion on their own, and who have trouble playing and interacting cooperatively with other children are exhibiting traits that may indicate a learning disorder will later be identified.

Once children are exposed to formal instruction, learning disabilities are usually manifested by hyperactivity and fidgeting, attentional lapses, easy distractibility, inability or unwillingness to complete assignments, and variability of performance (doing well on some tasks but much less well on others). More specifically, children with reading-related disabilities generally lack fluency, tend to reverse letters, and often lose their place in a book. Children with writing problems usually produce jerky and nearly unrecognizable letters, and take more time than most children to complete their work. Children who have problems with mathematics tend to have trouble memorizing math facts, struggle with positional notation (don't recognize that 10 represents "ten"), and have trouble with story problems. Clearly, if these sorts of learning difficulties are not attended to, the children who have them may build up a cumulative deficit of knowledge and skills as a result.

Curriculum-Disabled Children

When considering whether a child has a learning disability, it is important to remember that not all learning problems reside within the child. In my own work, I have identified many children who might be called *curriculum-disabled*. These are children of average ability who are functioning below the academic norm. In contrast to underachievers — who have the ability but not the needed motivation — curriculum-disabled children show many of the symptoms of learning-disabled children. The difference is that a curriculum-disabled child's problems are created by a mismatch between the curriculum and the child.

This occurs because in many schools the curriculum is still geared to a "universal child" and takes little if any account of differences in learning styles, growth rates and so on. And in many textbooks, the material is dull and written at the wrong level, the instructions are confusing, and the illustrations do not make the text more interesting or understandable.

As mentioned earlier, I once ran a school for curriculum-disabled children, The Mount Hope School in Rochester, NY. We took children from the public schools who seemed curriculum-disabled and kept them at our school for one or two years. In addition to doing regular classroom work, each child was tutored by a college student, who met with the child three times a week throughout the year. We tried to find appropriate ways to introduce the learning tasks to different students, and in most cases this resulted in the children returning to public schools at or above grade level.[2] Essentially, these children required a more custom-made curriculum than the one they had previously been offered.

Working with Learning- or Curriculum-Disabled Children

In working with curriculum-disabled children, as in working with children with all types of learning disabilities, I believe that there is one all-important rule to follow, which was also the rule that the college-age tutors found the hardest to put into practice. The rule is *to always approach the child at his or her own level*, not where the child is supposed to be on the basis of age or grade placement. For example, if a child of seven or eight does not know certain letters of the alphabet or basic numbers, that is where you have to start; you cannot insist that the child should be at his or her age level in respect to the ability to read or do math problems. This is not coddling the child; it is simply meeting the child at his or her level, which is where the child is most likely to achieve success and start making meaningful progress.

Providing a tutor for a child with learning disabilities is also very helpful and can give the child the best possible chance of making good progress. The tutor might be an older student, a parent or grandparent, or a community volunteer, but what is important is that the tutor make a commitment to continue working with the child for at least a year. Even if the tutor meets only once a week with the child, this can make an enormous difference, because it gives the child a feeling that he or she is important enough for the tutor to spend a lot of time with, and this feeling can be just as helpful as the actual tutoring.

Attention Deficit/Hyperactivity Disorder

A new learning disability identified only recently is an *Attention Deficit/Hyperactivity Disorder* (ADHD). This complex syndrome can have genetic, physiological, neurological, psychological, and even sociological determinants. Overall, close to one-third of the children with other learning disabilities can also be diagnosed as ADHD.

In the Diagnostic Manual of the American Psychiatric Association, ADHD children are divided into three groups.[3] The first group of children, identified as predominantly *inattentive*, have trouble concentrating and are forgetful as well as easily and frequently distracted. A second group of children, described as predominantly *hyperactive-impulsive*, talk up a storm, are constantly on the move, and tend not to think before they act. The third group is made up of children who show a combination of the traits manifested by the other two groups.

Many ADHD children are treated with drugs such as Ritalin, but this type of medication must be used with care. First, the diagnosis should be made as certain as possible by eliminating other possible causes, such as environmental stress and family dysfunction. Then, family counseling and careful attention to dosage are also very important. Without these three components, the medication is likely to be misused. Of course, it is also important to remember that medication does not cure the problem, it only alleviates some of the symptoms that interfere with the child's ability to operate in a school environment.

An ADHD child's learning problems often seem secondary to more general behavioral characteristics, and as with children who have other learning disabilities, a classroom teacher can only do so much to accommodate an ADHD child's special needs. The teacher and student both need to receive additional support in order for the full range of needs in a classroom to be handled satisfactorily.

Behavior Disorders

The distinctions between learning disabilities, attentional disorders, and behavior disorders are not always clear and easy to identify. In general, children who have behavior disorders display *serious and persistent age-inappropriate behaviors that result in social conflict, personal unhappiness, and school failure.*[4] Because identifying children with behavior disorders is particularly difficult, there are no solid statistics as to the frequency of these disorders. A rough estimate would be that between 5 and 10 percent of today's school population display behavior problems serious enough to warrant special treatment.

Behavior problems generally fall into two groups. Some children deal with their problems through *internalization* and may therefore report a variety of psychosomatic illnesses, such as headaches and stomachaches. These children may also be fearful and anxious, lack self-confidence, and display symptoms of depression, such as self-derogatory remarks. Other children deal with their emotional problems by means of *externalization*. They may act out their problems by taunting, bullying, and engaging in malicious and destructive behavior. Studies have shown that externalization is one of the most persistent behavior traits and that children who persistently act out when young are likely to continue this behavior pattern throughout their lives.

In the past, many of these sorts of behavior problems were usually seen in the later grades only. Today, however, we see them not only in the primary schools, but even in preschool. There are probably a variety of reasons for this, including the fact that family disruption is much more common today than it was in the modern era, and this is extremely stressful for children. In addition, televised violence can also influence children who may be inclined to use externalization as a mode of dealing with their problems. And schools may also share some of the responsibility, as intense pressure created by academics, homework and grading at an early age can add to the other stresses children are experiencing. In many cases, a child may be able to deal with one or another of these stresses singly, but when too many different stresses coincide, the child's adaptive mechanisms break down, and he or she begins to engage in defensive behaviors.

The best way to deal with behavior problems is to focus on the most immediate and obvious contributors first. Sometimes, for example, a classroom may contains a bad mix of children, some of whom reinforce one another's aggressive tendencies and happen to have some ready victims in the same room. In other situations, the classroom frames have not been established strongly enough, and children who are so disposed take liberties, in which case the teacher needs to "tighten the reins." In a few cases, there may just be a personality clash between the teacher and child that needs to be addressed.

Some writers have encouraged parents and teachers to use a "time-out" technique with children who have disruptive behavior problems. The theory is that isolating the child will provide an opportunity to reflect upon and correct inappropriate behavior. But this actually misreads the situation. A child who is disruptive is asking for attention to his or her feelings and needs, and isolating the child reinforces the feeling that no one is being attentive. Disruptive children really need what psychologist Otto Weininger calls "time in" — someone to sit with the child and listen to his or her concerns and feelings.[5] This sort of social interaction attends to the child's true needs better than isolation.

For serious and prolonged behavior problems, however, the classroom teacher must have outside help from the school psychologist or social worker. And when preschool children display symptoms of a behavior disorder, the parents must be talked to and encouraged to obtain some professional help for their child. As with learning disabilities, emotional problems do not disappear —they tend to grow worse if not attended to. There are a number of different therapeutic approaches that can be effective, ranging from the psychoanalytic to the behavioral, and many appear quite similar in practice despite their different theoretical underpinnings.

During the modern era, it was customary to "locate" behavior problems in the child and treat the child in isolation from the rest of the family. This is still the approach used as part of many directive therapies that emphasize modifying specific behaviors. A newer, postmodern approach to behavior disorders, in contrast, recognizes that the child's problem is likely to be a reflection of family dynamics. Rather than focusing just on the child, therefore, this sort of approach treats the whole family and seeks to reorganize family interactions so as to reduce the stresses on the child.[6]

Developing Successful Inclusion Strategies

In the preceding pages, we reviewed the range of children who have special needs that now need to be met in our schools. The most pressing questions for educators and parents of these children are whether and how different children's special needs can be met through inclusion, which is now the prevalent strategy for educating special-needs children.

Inclusion remains controversial among educators and parents. Some people argue that all children with special needs can be included successfully in a regular classroom, and that all the other children in the classroom also benefit from this approach. Other people believe that some children who have special needs require individualized teaching techniques that might not be necessary for other children, who can benefit from certain group-oriented techniques that would not be appropriate or effective for some of the special-needs children.

Years of experience with inclusion have tended to show that the real issue is not whether inclusion is right or wrong, but rather *under what circumstances inclusion is likely to be successful*. This postmodern perspective recognizes that rather than one universal solution, the ultimate success or failure of inclusion depends on a number of variables that may differ widely in particular situations. Educators and parents should therefore consider these specific variables — and their cumulative effect — when considering the inclusion of special-needs children:

1. The teacher-to-child ratio. Clearly, a teacher who has 16 children in her classroom will have more time to meet all her students' individual needs than a teacher who has a class of 25.

2. The percentage of children who have special needs. There are no clear research-based guidelines on the issue, but it seems highly likely that as the percentage of special-needs children increases, the time available to meet those needs decreases. Not only does this mean that the classroom requires additional support, it also increases the likelihood that the children who do not have special needs (and their parents) will feel that their needs are not being met, because so much of the teacher's time is being taken up by needs that are highly individual.

3. The types of special needs. A classroom teacher may find it fairly easy to include several children who have reading or other language problems, but even two children with severe visual disabilities or cerebral palsy might make inclusion a far more difficult task. Again, there is no clear research on this issue, and much depends on the specific teacher and the support services available.

4. The developmental levels of the children who have disabilities. In addition to the impact of a disability on a child's academic performance, educators and parents also have a responsibility to consider the child's overall intellectual, physical, and social/emotional development. When any of these aspects of development are out of sync with those of the other students in a class, the child is likely to need far more of the teacher's attention, including individualized instruction.

5. The level of teacher training and other preparations for including special-needs children. Teacher-training programs around the country vary greatly in the degree to which they prepare teachers to include special-needs children in a class. Until recently, children who have special needs were a teaching specialty, and many teachers expecting to be in regular classrooms took few — if any — courses dealing with special needs. Accordingly, a teacher's previous training, along with other preparations to

149

include special-needs children, cannot be taken for granted.

6. The preparation of the special-needs child for inclusion. Not all children are equally ready to participate in a regular classroom. A child who has special needs and has only received individualized attention, having never been in a large-group educational environment, may find the switch to such a setting quite stressful. In this situation, the child is likely to benefit from being introduced to the classroom gradually rather than all at once, and from having time to work through the anxiety caused by separating from a primary caregiver.

7. The availability of resource specialists. This is an extremely important variable, because resource specialists not only have expertise in working with children's disabilities, they also free some of the teacher's time for working with the other children. In addition, both the teacher and student benefit from the teacher's ability to consult a trained professional who also works with the child. And resources specialists can be a great morale booster because they can help the teacher feel less alone and frustrated.

Conclusion

The inclusion of special-needs children in a regular classroom can have many benefits for all the children, if it is done wisely and well. Considering the variables mentioned above can help adults arrive at reasonable, common-sense decisions that reflect the different needs of children in particular situations. The special-needs children can then benefit from their involvement with other children, who, in turn, become better prepared for life in our diverse society. This aspect of the postmodern reinvention of childhood, in which the different and irregular come to be considered normal, can serve us all well as we continue our efforts to adapt to the changes in our society and our world.

Chapter 8

The Ongoing Process of Reinventing Childhood

Reinvention, like invention itself, is an ongoing effort at problem solving. As such, reinvention necessarily involves a great deal of trial and error as well as — hopefully — some creative insights. Knowing that many of our postmodern attempts at reinventing are still in progress, I want to conclude this book by reviewing several of these ongoing efforts in order to see how effectively they are meeting the needs of today's children, and also to see what we can learn from them and apply to other aspects of the reinvention of childhood.

In addition, this review will give me an opportunity to offer my own evaluations and suggestions, which will be based on the following general principle. *From my perspective, the most effective reinventions of childhood are those that incorporate the best of both the modern and postmodern insights about childhood.* At its most essential level, this means combining the modern emphasis on differences between age levels with the postmodern emphasis on differences between children of the same age.

With this in mind, I would like to review ongoing reinventions in three key domains. The first is *educational* and will be illustrated by different approaches to reinventing first grade and its students. The second is *technological*, and in this regard reinvention will be illustrated by efforts to reinvent children as educational television viewers and computer users. Lastly, in the *clinical* domain, we will examine the reinvention of children as needing self-esteem, quality time, and time-outs.

153

Reinventing Young Children as Academic Learners

The 1960s were a period of tumultuous change for our society, and one of the lasting results has been a new attention to early childhood education. The women's movement and the growing financial pressures on families increased the social acceptance of out-of-home work by the mothers of young children, And, the civil rights movement led to a recognition of the importance of early childhood as a period in which disadvantaged children, in particular, need intellectual stimulation and other types of preparation for school. This all led to a rapid expansion of day care and preschool programs for young children, ranging from the federally mandated Head Start programs to nationwide chains of child care centers owned by large corporations.

Due to this rapid expansion, by the mid-1990s some 85 percent of the children entering kindergarten had already been in some sort of out-of-home program. However, these programs vary widely as to the quality of the care, intellectual stimulation, and social/emotional guidance they provide. Due to this and other changes in the postmodern society and its families, the children coming to public schools today display a far greater range of intellectual and social/emotional skills than was typical in the past.

Despite this variability, however, in many schools first grade has been reinvented as a place where entering students have already acquired basic reading and math skills. This is based on the idea that the increased preschool attendance, combined with exposure to television programs such as *Sesame Street* that attempt to teach elementary number and letter recognition, have enabled children to learn these skills at younger ages than in the past. In addition, the pressure to have children meet high-level standards in elementary school has also encour-

154

aged this sort of attempt to teach children more and expect more from them at an earlier age.

Nonetheless, many children entering first grade have not acquired basic reading and math skills, which used to be part of the first-grade curriculum rather than a prerequisite for it. Due to this lack of skills, which may also be combined with a lack of the social/emotional skills needed to work productively in first grade, many kindergartners are not being promoted along with their age mates. To accommodate these children, a number of different approaches are being used.

One is the time-honored practice of *retention* — having children repeat a grade — which has recently been used with increasing frequency. For some children, remaining in kindergarten for another year is, indeed, the "least worst" choice. Still, the decision to retain a kindergartner should be made with care and take into account the child's maturity, the intellectual demands of the first grade in question, and the child's own feelings about the matter. I recall discussing the issue of retention with one 5-year-old, who decided to stay with a kindergarten teacher she liked. One of the reasons was that a girl who had "glommed onto her" during the year was moving on to first grade.

Like inclusion and other widely used educational practices, retention is neither bad nor good in principle. Rather, it may be good or bad for different children in particular situations. Much like the social, emotional, motor, and intellectual maturity of the incoming children, first grades vary widely as to their methods and level of instruction, so a retention decision should depend primarily on the fit between the child and the class he or she will be entering.

Another way to accommodate children who don't fit the mold of the reinvented first grader is to place them in a *transition class*, which usually has a combination of kindergarten and first-grade features. After a year in this class, the children then move on to first grade, and as with retention, the decision to

155

place a child in such a class should only be made after considering the particular class and the individual child. If the class is small, if it has not become a "dumping ground" for children with non-academic problems, and if the teacher is well trained, the transition class can be an excellent choice for children who are not yet ready for first grade. Even if these conditions are met, however, the child's feelings still need to be considered. If the child views being in a transition class as a sign of failure, or if he or she desperately wants to be with peers in a regular classroom, these personal feelings need to be taken seriously. The very best transition class may not benefit a child who resents the placement, so the decision always has to be made on an individual basis.

A third way to accommodate children who are not yet ready for first grade is through *multi-age grouping*. With this approach, children at two or three age levels are brought together in the same classroom. For example, a multi-age classroom might have both kindergarten and first-grade students, or both first and second-grade students. Such groupings, reminiscent of the one-room school house, have a number of advantages. For one thing, only one half or a third of the children are new to the classroom each year, and this eases their incorporation into the group. Secondly, a teacher gets to know the children better over a two-or three-year period and can better adapt the curriculum to each student's individual needs and abilities. Thirdly, this can make it easier for some children to work with others who have the same ability level, even though their age levels differ.

As with the other options, multi-age grouping is not a cure-all and presents its own challenges. Most teachers have not been trained to work with a group of children who have such widely different skill levels, which can make the work daunting and the teacher less effective. Also, in some cases, having the same teacher with children for two or three years can become a problem if there is a mismatch between the personalities. Finally, some parents worry that the academic standards for older children will be lowered and the curriculum "dumbed down" because of the younger children in the same room. These are not insurmountable obstacles, but dedication, hard work, and innovative teaching strategies are clearly needed to make a multi-age classroom successful.

Retention, multi-age grouping, and, to some extent, transition classes were all used during the modern era and reflected an implicit recognition of variations among children within the same age group. During the postmodern era, these practices have become more widespread, as our recognition of differences among same-age children has increased. And as I have tried to make clear, all three approaches can be used to address the particularity and irregularity of individual children, if placement decisions are not made on general principles but are instead based on careful evaluation of both the child and the classroom. In other words, *readiness is not solely within the child — it should always refer to the match between the child and the classroom.*

Reinventing Young Children as Educational Technology Users

Young Children as Educational Television Viewers

The advent and pervasive impact of television has led to a number of different reinventions of children as television viewers. This can be seen in the different approaches to educating young children through public television shows as diverse as *Sesame Street* and *Mr. Rogers' Neighborhood*, which seem to make quite different assumptions about the young children who watch them. Comparing these different approaches can help us understand how television is being adapted to meet young children's needs, and how children are adapting to different types of television.

Mr. Rogers' Neighborhood approaches young children as if television viewing is much the same as playing or interacting with parents. The show focuses on issues such as being liked, getting along with other children, learning how objects and artwork are created, and enjoying play and fantasy. By doing things such as changing his shoes and putting on a sweater when he walks in the door at the start of each show, Mr. Rogers tries to make his television program an extension of the child's home.

Moreover, Mr. Rogers makes no attempt to teach academics. Instead, he emphasizes helping children deal with everyday experiences and with their feelings, including common fears and anxieties. In this respect, and in its pacing, tone, language, and style, *Mr. Rogers' Neighborhood* is well suited to the young child described by Freud and other modern grandmasters. On the other hand, this program is quite postmodern in presenting children who have different cultural backgrounds, skin color and special needs. Overall, the program therefore represents an effective integration of the modern and postmodern perspectives on young children.

Still, *Mr. Rogers' Neighborhood* is not without its critics. One mother told me she never lets her son watch Mr. Rogers because he is too nice to be a good masculine role model for her son. In addition, the lack of emphasis on academic skills worries some parents. If children are spending time watching educational television, they argue, shouldn't the time be used to teach academic as well as social/emotional skills? For reasons such as these, the particular integration of the modern and postmodern that Mr. Rogers provides is not acceptable to all postmodern parents.

Sesame Street, in contrast, started from the premise that young children are avid learners, and that television provides a unique medium that can be both informative and enjoyable. And as Naomi Baron explains, it has become a means of teaching academic content to young children:

"*Sesame Street* has done more to redefine literacy goals for young children than any other single force since education became compulsory in America. Goals designed for 5-year-olds are frequently reached by 3- and even 2-year-olds. Viewers as young as twelve months may spend several hours daily watching intently, thanks to repeat programming, multiple public broadcasting channels and the wonder of VCRs. Such intense viewing from an early age can significantly accelerate the beginning stages of literacy."[1]

Sesame Street thus meets the demands of parents who believe that children's television should be directly instructive as well as entertaining. And over the years, *Sesame Street* has evolved in ways that meet the needs of younger children, by slowing its pace and making some of its material more developmentally appropriate. But while Naomi Baron affirms that the show has helped young children learn letters and numbers, she also notes that it does not teach them to read or do arithmetic, which require more systematic instruction.

Some critics of *Sesame Street* have even questioned whether the intensive viewing of fast-paced and colorful audio/visual material by young children makes it more difficult for them to learn to read black-and-white print and work with silent, stationary numbers a few years later. As Clifford Stoll writes,

"*Sesame Street* has been around for twenty years. Indeed, its idea of making learning relevant to all was as widely promoted in the seventies as the internet is today.

So where's that demographic wave of creative and brilliant students now entering college?...Did we inflate their expectations that learning would always be colorful and fun?"[2]

In comparing *Sesame Street* with *Mr. Rogers' Neighborhood*, therefore, we can see two different approaches to reinventing the child as a viewer of educational television. *Mr. Rogers' Neighborhood* accepts the basic character of the young child as defined during the modern era, and uses television as a new and powerful way of addressing the young child's traditional needs and concerns. *Sesame Street* is designed to engage children and bring out new abilities and interests that remained latent in the modern child, because there seemed to be no effective way to elicit them. In this respect, the introduction of *Sesame Street* resembles Montessori's introduction of child-sized chairs, tables and implements, which enabled children to accomplish tasks they could not have completed with adult-sized objects.

In evaluating educational television and other new media, we need to consider how well it has been adapted to the known needs and abilities of young children, as well as how it can be used to help young children realize hitherto latent capacities. *Mr. Rogers' Neighborhood* focuses on meeting the first challenge, while *Sesame Street* focuses on meeting the second. The remaining challenge is to find some way to combine the strengths of both these approaches.

Young Children as Educational Computer Users

The history of education is replete with predictions of how new technologies would totally transform the way children learn. Thomas Edison predicted in 1922 that motion pictures would quickly replace textbooks. About a quarter of a century later, the newly invented, battery-operated radio was expected to replace the blackboard. Then, in the 1960s, B.F. Skinner claimed that his teaching machines, built on his principles of reinforcement, would double the efficiency of classroom learning. Today, school closets may still contain overhead projectors, reel-to-reel cassettes, and combined film projectors/cassette

160

players, as well as some old Apple IIs, Commodore 64s, and PC Juniors gathering dust.

This is not to say that computers are necessarily the next in a long line of failed or obsolete educational technologies; only that we need to keep their potential benefits in perspective, especially where young children are concerned. One of the problems educators now face is simply the wide range of computer programs created for young children. Another is that all these programs necessarily present the young child with a learning experience that is *symbolic* (whether based on pictures, icons, letters, or numbers) and *mediated* (through a keyboard and/or mouse). Young children, however, still need to spend most of their time working with and constructing their own conceptions of forms, qualities, and objects through direct, multi-sensory experiences.

While it may be that computers can actualize some hitherto latent intellectual capacities in the young child, as *Sesame Street* may have done, this has yet to be demonstrated. In a comprehensive 1997 review article about computers in education, Todd Oppenheimer presents a lot of evidence that challenges the major claims of those who want to make computer literacy a top priority in our schools.[3]

For example, Seymour Papert's Logo program was supposed to promote procedural thinking in young children by having them learn elementary computer programming.[4] To date, however, the research data does not support this proposition. Nor is there evidence that working with the "hypertext" capabilities of computers helps children develop minds that operate in parallel rather than sequential fashion. Indeed, many psychologists believe that just the reverse is true, with computers exercising the left (sequential) part of the brain at the expense of the right (creative) half.

Of particular relevance to early childhood education is the argument that children need to be trained on computers as early as possible so as not to be put at a disadvantage. According to

161

Oppenheimer, a lead technology adviser in the Department of Education thinks "that there is no particular minimum age — and no maximum number of hours — that children should spend on a terminal." Nor has this adviser seen any examples of excess.

Perhaps Jane Healy put it best in regard to young children spending too much time watching television or working with computers:

> "Unproven technologies...may offer lively visions, but they can also be detrimental to the development of the young plastic brain. The cerebral cortex is a wondrously well-buffered mechanism that can withstand a good bit of well-intentioned bungling. Yet there is a point at which fundamental neural substrates for reasoning may be jeopardized for children who lack proper physical, intellectual and emotional nurturance. Childhood — and the brain — have their own imperatives. In development, missed opportunities may be difficult to recapture."[5]

It is interesting to note that this paragraph could easily have been written by Maria Montessori or Jean Piaget. It restates, from a postmodern neuropsychological perspective, their views regarding the importance of real sensory/motor experience for the healthy intellectual development of the young child.

Over time, computers may indeed make significant improvements in some of the ways we educate young children, if we discover new methods of instruction that were not possible without computers. For example, virtual reality might be used to overcome the motivational problems with learning a foreign language, if the technology could "transport" young children to another country where they were surrounded by the language and needed to use it to reach a goal. We are, however, not there yet.

Even with such innovations, computers will certainly not eliminate the need for human teachers. Early childhood education, in particular, is and always will be primarily a matter of interpersonal interaction. Consider this vignette about a child working with Apple's Early Learning Connection program:

> "On a typical day, 5-year-old Peter works at a computer in his kindergarten classroom. 'Let me show you what I can do,' he says, as he takes the mouse, points at the Kidworks 2 folder and opens the program. He then selects the drawing option, picks out a clip art scene, and begins creating an illustration of the story he's composed."[6]

What is significant about this vignette is that the child starts out by saying, "Let me show you what I can do." As John Dewey said, learning is the representation of experience, and this child is motivated not just to work on the computer but also to show the teacher how he does so. Young children such as Peter may indeed be learning from the computer, but they still need to be involved with real-world materials and knowledgeable, caring adults. *Learning is first and foremost a social activity, and machines of whatever wizardry will never equal the magic of a competent, caring teacher.*

Reinventing Young Children's Social and Emotional Needs

Changes in our postmodern society and its families have raised new social and emotional issues for children. The value now placed on the autonomy of family members has helped to focus attention on children's sense of *self-esteem*. The emphasis on autonomy, combined with the large number of singe-parent families and families in which both parents work, has also led to concerns about the amount of *quality time* family members spend together. And the need to deal with children's social and emotional problems in the midst of the many other demands on adults' time has, in part, led to the practice of using *time-outs*.

While all these aspects of the reinvention of childhood have merit, they tend to emphasize the solitary — rather than the social —nature of childhood, so in the following sections I will include suggestions for balancing children's individual and social needs.

Reinventing Children's Self-Esteem

It is not clear exactly where and how the tremendous concern about postmodern children's self-esteem developed, but certainly one prominent contributor was child psychologist Haim Ginott. In his best-selling book *Between Parent and Child*, he argued that the language we use can affect children's self-esteem, and we should therefore avoid language that has a negative impact on it.[7] One technique he suggested was that we distinguish between what one of his students labeled "I Messages" and "You Messages." Parents were urged to use phrasing such as "It makes me feel good when you put things away," rather than "How many times have I told you not to leave your things in such a mess?"

Clearly, Ginott did us all a service by pointing out that we sometimes make children feel bad about themselves because of our inadvertent or insensitive use of language. As adults, we know that words can hurt and that children are often far more sensitive than we to pain caused by harsh or cruel language, so we need to find supportive and effective ways to discuss problems. At the same time, we also have to be sensitive to the differences in children's ages and the effect those differences have on children's understanding of language. The importance of these differences has sometimes been downplayed or overlooked in an effort to make all children feel good about themselves.

For example, Ginott suggests that when an adult responds to children's artwork, he or she should say something like "It makes me feel good when I look at your painting." The reason for this is that a child's painting can easily be misinterpreted, with an adult saying, "Oh, I like your parrot," when the child was drawing something else entirely. Yet there is also a risk to emphasizing that a young child's actions make an adult feel good, because young children often engage in "magical thinking," which leads them to believe that their thoughts affect other people and events. By frequently using the phrase "It makes me feel good when you...," adults may encourage a young child to believe that he or she deserves the credit or blame for adults' other moods and actions. Verbal techniques such as these should therefore be carefully matched to the particular situation and age of the child, rather than used as a standard formula.

The emphasis on using supportive language has been part of a larger trend to place undue emphasis on children's self-esteem, to the point that it came to be viewed as a key component of some schools' curriculum and of children's mental health in general. In part, this has resulted from a recognition that too many postmodern children are growing up in more difficult circumstances than children of the modern era. Yet psychologists are not even sure exactly what self-esteem is. Questions remain as to whether self-esteem is one thing or many, whether the child develops it internally or from interactions with others, and so on.

More importantly, the idea that we should never hurt a child's self-esteem has also been misinterpreted to mean that children should always feel good about themselves. But when children make mistakes or even deliberately say or do hurtful things, feeling guilty or bad about these things can be a healthy part of their development. These feelings can help us think before we act as well as refrain from doing something hurtful again.

This is an area where one of the modern grandmasters still has something to teach us. In discussing the psychosexual stages of development, Erik Erikson suggests that self-esteem incorporates feelings of trust, autonomy, initiative, identity, intimacy, generativity, and integrity.[8] He also argues that at every stage of development, a balance between positive and negative senses of

165

self is the most healthy outcome. At the preschool level, for example, children need to develop some sense of guilt to balance an overweening sense of initiative.

Providing only positive feedback and letting children develop an inflated sense of self-esteem does them a disservice. *In order for children to develop in a healthy manner, they need to be able to distinguish between good and bad, especially in regard to their own actions.*

Reinventing Parent-Child Interactions

The time pressures on postmodern parents are extraordinary. Jeremy Rifkin has called this phenomenon a "time famine," and Arlie Hochschild talks about the "time bind." In large part, these time pressures result from the increase in the number of single-parent families and families in which both parents work, as well as the demands of an ever-changing technological workplace and global economy, all of which limit the amount of time parents can spend with their children. When these factors are combined with the increased value adults place on their own autonomy, it is not surprising that an important aspect of the reinvention of childhood has been an attempt to compensate for the effects of all these time pressures on parent-child relationships.

One approach to this issue has been the development of the concept that the amount of time children spend with their parents is less important than the *quality* of that time. The phrase "quality time" has become widely used during the postmodern era, as books and articles advise parents on ways to compensate for the reduced amount of time they are spending with their children. Yet the quality of the time parents spend with their children is not easy to measure or even define. Does quality time include doing chores with a child, or is it only going to a ball game or engaging in some other enjoyable activity? And if conflicts or a need for disciplining arises during this time, is it still quality time? Perhaps even more importantly, how much quality time is needed to make up for several hours of out-of-home day care or television watching with a baby sitter?

Questions such as these need clear answers in order for the concept of quality time to withstand close examination. In addition, the need for quality time is based in part on a somewhat nostalgic idealization of the modern family. In the early part of the twentieth century, for example, the working day for fathers was usually longer, and while mothers were more likely to stay at home, they usually had more children to care for, and there were far fewer labor-saving devices, so household chores took more time. These factors also limited the amount of time parents could spend with their children, and because neighborhoods were deemed safe, children were often just told to "go out and play." By the 1950s, these circumstances had changed for many middle-class American families, but this proved to be a relatively brief respite before the changes of the 1960s and 1970s began to alter family life and employment once again.

What children did receive in the modern family — and what they do not experience as much today — has little to do with either the quantity or quality of time spent together. What was different in the modern era was that children had substantial evidence that *parents were willing to make sacrifices on their behalf.*

Let me give a personal example. When I was growing up, my father was a machinist who often worked ten-hour shifts, as well as on Saturdays. By the time he came home, he was exhausted. We never played ball, never went fishing, never engaged in any of the "quality time" activities that are now being promoted. (I did occasionally help him when he did repairs around the house, and that is when he taught me how to use tools.) Nonetheless, my brothers and sisters and I deeply loved and respected my father. He spent virtually nothing on himself and worked very hard to give us everything we needed to achieve a better life. His example of honesty, decency, caring, and selflessness was far more meaningful than any type of quality time.

It is this evidence that parents are willing to make sacrifices on a child's behalf that is the true basis of an unshakable sense of self-worth and self-esteem, because it shows how much the parents care about the child and how important the child is in their lives. Of course, many postmodern parents continue to make sacrifices in order to spend time with their children. They may leave work early or skip an adult-oriented event to go to a ball game or recital. But it is not just their physical presence that is important to the child; it is also the knowledge that the parents gave up a valued adult activity to be there for the child.

As parents, we can show our children how important they are in other ways. If we have to travel on business, one of the most rewarding things we can do is to write children a letter. Phone calls are great, but a letter is something a child can keep and read again and again. Moreover, letter writing takes solitary time and thought, which also convey a sense of sacrifice to the child. (Of course, a letter also reinforces the value of reading and writing.) We also show this type of caring when we buy our children things that show we took the time to listen, observe, and discover what they really wanted. These may seem like little, routine things, but they can mean a lot.

Although the classroom is very different from the home, and teachers are not parents, students still benefit from knowing that teachers regard them as important. Ironically, one of the ways we can do this is by establishing rules and frames, and then following through with the penalties we set for breaking the rules or deliberately spoiling a frame. This is a sacrifice because it is much easier not to set rules and mete out penalties, and students do realize that taking these steps shows we care enough to make these efforts on their behalf. As one child said when a teacher made no effort to control a few students who were acting up, "I guess she doesn't really care about us, or she wouldn't let them get away with that stuff."

The idea of sacrificing for children was implicit in many of the practices suggested by the crafters of modern childhood. When Montessori created child-sized chairs, tables, and implements, she was sacrificing adult convenience and making an exceptional effort that showed how much she cared about children. In the same way, giving up the ease and simplicity of direct instruction for the more difficult teaching practice of listening to children and following their leads is another kind of sacrifice. In short, whenever we adopt developmentally appropriate practices, we sacrifice adult comfort and convenience so as to adapt to the needs and interests of children. In so doing we give children the unshakable conviction that they are important in our lives.

Reinventing Discipline

Sending children to their bedroom or to the corner of a classroom or to some other separate location has long been a standard disciplinary technique. In the postmodern era, with its emphasis on formalizing, defining and using techniques, this approach is now widely used and has been refined into what is now known as a *time-out*. Here's an example of how the author of a book advised parents to use this technique with an 8-year-old who had lost control:

> "The specific intervention I recommended was the nonpunitive time-out: moving an excited youngster to more quiet surroundings. Unlike an ordinary time-out, used as an after-the-fact punishment, this helps a child calm down. The adult is sympathetic; the child does not have to be isolated or deprived of his privileges; he can read, watch TV or socialize quietly.
>
> I suggested that Kevin's parents have a planned discussion with him to explain what they would be doing. It is important to let him know that the time-out is not a punishment but a way of helping him. Part of a

169

collaborative approach is teaching Kevin about himself and pointing out signs of over-excitement that he can watch for. Ideally, Kevin will learn to give himself a time-out when he senses his control is slipping."[9]

Time-outs can be effective for some children and in certain situations, and they may help to teach children self-control, but this is not necessarily the case. We always need to assess the child and the situation before using any particular disciplinary technique. Specifically, some children who are acting up and out of control need adult support and interaction, rather than isolation. In his book entitled *Time-Ins*, Dr. Otto Weininger argues that at least some children who are acting up need a *"time-in,"* during which an adult sits with them and actively helps them gain mastery over their feelings.[10]

Dr. Weininger suggests that parents can do this by sharing their own emotional control with a child who is angry, unhappy, willful, or upset. If the parent does not grow upset at the child's behavior, and if the parent stays with the child and verbalizes the child's feelings, the child can feel comforted and develop a sense of control. In part, what a child learns during a time-in is that adults are not afraid of the child's emotions and are able to handle them. This gives the child the wonderful reassurance that he or she can master these emotions as well.

In many ways, time-outs are a postmodern reinvention tied to the sense of a child's autonomy and self-reflective capabilities, whereas time-ins are modern in that they reflect the idea that children need adults to serve as models of emotional control. But just as with time-outs, the use of time-ins has to be individualized. Time-outs may work well for children who are usually well-behaved but lose control because of over-stimulation. In contrast, children who have continuing emotional problems may benefit more from time-ins with supportive adults. *In practice, both time-outs and time-ins can be useful strategies when they are appropriate for the particular child and situation.*

Conclusion

We have now looked at some of the ongoing reinventions of childhood in regard to education, educational technologies, and children's social and emotional needs. As I have tried to demonstrate at various points throughout this chapter and the book, the most successful postmodern reinventions incorporate the modern insights about the regularity of age differences with the postmodern appreciation of differences among same-age children.

The resulting reinvention of childhood is one that sympathetically acknowledges the ways individual children are different, while accepting their common humanity. And this concept of childhood also recognizes, as noted at the start of this book, that while the experience and perception of childhood have changed markedly during the postmodern era, children's basic capabilities and needs remain much the same as they were decades and even centuries ago.

Reinventing Developmentally Appropriate Practice

The principle of developmentally appropriate practice reflects the modern conception of the child, in that it prescribes that educational practice be suited to children's developing capacities and interests. Although this is a modern idea first introduced by Rousseau in his classic *Emile* and implicit in the work of the grandmasters, it did not become a widely accepted principle until the late 20th century. Unfortunately, it is still often misunderstood as a curriculum mandate, rather than as a demand for thoughtful analysis and the matching of curriculum content with children's changing capacities and interests.

Now that we have moved into the postmodern era, our conception of childhood has changed and so too must our principle of developmentally appropriate practice. This does not mean that we must give up the effort to match curriculum and development, but that instead we need to couple this with a sensitive respect for individual differences. Put differently, *developmentally appropriate practice must be coupled with individually appropriate practice.*

Clearly, a developmentally appropriate activity for most 5-year-olds may not be appropriate for a 5-year-old who has cerebral palsy. In the same way, a dyslexic 6-year-old may need to be taught in a different way than classmates who do not have this type of disability. Similar considerations hold for the full range of individual differences discussed in this book.

This integration of developmentally and individually appropriate practice results in what I would call *vital teaching*, just as schools that incorporate both principles could be called *vital schools*. Such practice and schools are vital in the sense that they are essential, energetic, and supportive of growth.

Vital teaching and schools are needed in a democracy, because they encourage both individual autonomy and social responsibility in a harmonious way. And this approach cannot be limited just to students. Vital schools foster the personal and professional growth of educators as well, because vital teaching requires educators to be careful observers and enthusiastic learners, as well as accurate guides and caring mentors.

In a similar way, families also need to meet the individual and social needs of both children and parents. And they need to prepare young people to become responsible and productive members of our democratic society. My hope, therefore, is that we will increasingly create and become part of *vital families*, which meet the developmental and personal needs of all their members.

With a postmodern perspective attuned to individual differences as well as the differences between age groups, we have the understanding needed to create vital schools and vital families. These schools and families will offer the best opportunities for children to become unique and valued members of our society.

References

Preface

Elkind, D. *The Hurried Child*. Reading, MA: Addison Wesley, 1981/1988.

Elkind, D. *Miseducation*. New York: Knopf, 1984.

Elkind, D. *All Grown Up and No Place to Go*. Reading, MA: Addison Wesley, 1984/1998.

Postman, N. *The Disappearance of Childhood*. New York: Delacorte, 1983.

Winn, M. *Children Without Childhood*. New York: Pantheon, 1983.

Chapter 1

1. Freud, S. *The Basic Writings of Sigmund Freud*. New York: Modern Library, 1938.
2. Elkind, D. *Ties That Stress*. Cambridge, MA: Harvard University Press, 1994.
3. Lasch, C. *Haven in a Heartless World*. New York: Norton, 1977.
4. Chukovsky, K. *From Two to Five*. Berkeley, CA: University of California Press, 1968.
5. Taylor, A.R. *The Study of the Child*. New York: Appleton, 1899.
6. Froebel, F. *Pedagogics of the Kindergarten*. New York: Appleton, 1895.
7. Montessori, M. *The Montessori Method*. New York: Shocken, 1912/1964.
8. Freud, S. *The Basic Writings of Sigmund Freud*. New York: Modern Library, 1938.
9. Piaget, J. *The Psychology of Intelligence*. London: Routledge & Kegan Paul, 1950.
10. Nietzsche, F. *Human, All Too Human*. New York: Cambridge University Press, 1986.
11. Wittgenstein, L. *Letters from Ludwig Wittgenstein with a Memoir*. New York: Oxford University Press, 1967.
12. Kierkegaard, S. *Stages on Life's Way*. Princeton, NJ: Princeton University Press, 1945.
13. Brazelton, T.B. *Touchpoints*. Reading, MA: Addison Wesley, 1994.
14. Leach, P. *Babyhood: From Birth to Age Two*. New York: Knopf, 1976.

Chapter 2

1. Froebel, F. *Pedagogics of the Kindergarten*. New York: Appleton, 1895.
2. Brosterman, N. *Inventing Kindergarten*. New York: Abrams, 1997.
3. Montessori, M. *The Montessori Method*. New York: Schocken, 1916/64.
4. Montessori, M. *The Absorbent Mind*. New York: Dell, 1967.
5. Freud, S. *The Basic Writings of Sigmund Freud*. New York: Modern Library, 1938.
6. Steiner, R. *The Roots of Education*. London: Rudolf Steiner Press, 1968.
7. Piaget, J. *The Language and Thought of the Child*. London: Routledge & Kegan Paul, 1942.
8. Piaget, J. *The Psychology of Intelligence*. London: Routledge & Kegan Paul, 1950.
9. Inhelder, B. and J. Piaget. *The Growth of Logical Thinking from Childhood to Adolescence*. New York: Basic Books, 1958.
10. Kozulin, A. *Vygotsky's Psychology*. Cambridge, MA: Harvard University Press, 1990.
11. Vygotsky, L. *Mind in Society*. Cambridge, MA: Harvard University Press, 1978.
— Vygotsky, L. *Thought and Language*. Cambridge, MA: The MIT Press, 1962.
12. Bodrova, E. and D. Leong. *Tools of the Mind*. Englewood Cliffs, NJ: Prentice Hall, 1996.
13. West, J. and E. Hausken. *Approaching Kindergarten: A Look at Preschoolers in the United States* [Statistical Analysis Report]. Washington, DC: US Department of Education: Office of Educational Research and Improvement, 1995.
14. Erikson, E. *Childhood and Society*. New York: Norton, 1950.

Chapter 3

1. Chamberlin, A. *The Child: A Sudy in the Evolution of Man*. London: Walter Scott, Ltd., 1900.
2. Gesell, A. *The First Five Years of Life*. New York: Harper & Row, 1940.
3. Piaget, J. *The Language and Thought of the Child*. London: Routledge & Kegan Paul, 1942.
4. Chomsky, N. *Language and Mind*. New York: Harcourt, Brace & World, 1968.
5. Lennenberg, E. *Biological Foundations of Language*. New York: Wiley, 1967.
6. Flesh, R. *Why Johnny Can't Read and What You Can do About It*. New York: Harper & Row, 1958.

7. Goodman, K. "The Key in Children's Language." *The Reading Teacher*, March, 1972.

8. Smith, F. *Understanding Reading*. New York: Holt, Rinehart and Winston, 1971.

9. Baron, N. *Growing Up with Language*. Reading, MA: Addison Wesley, 1992.

Chapter 4

1. Parsons, T. *Essays in Sociological Theory*. Glencoe, IL: The Free Press, 1949.

2. Furth, H. *Desire for Society*. New York: Plenum, 1996.

3. Goffman, E. *Frame Analysis*. New York: Harper & Row, 1974.

Chapter 5

1. Sheldon, W. and S. Stevens. *The Varieties of Temperament*. New York: Harper, 1942.

2. Jung, C. *Psychological Types*. Princeton, NJ: Princeton University Press, 1921/1953.

3. Thomas, A. and S. Chess. *Temperament and Development*. New York: Bruner/Mazel, 1974.

4. de Tocqueville, A. *Democracy in America (Volume 2)*. New York: Vintage, 1840/1990.

5. Kagan, J. "Reflective and Impulsive Children: Significance of Conceptual Tempo." In J.D. Krumholz (Ed.), *Learning and the Educational Process*. Chicago: Rand McNally, 1956.

6. Macoby, E. and C. Jacklin. *The Psychology of Sex Differences*. Palo Alto, CA: Stanford University Press, 1974.

7. Kohlberg, L. "The Cognitive Developmental Approach to Moral Education." *Phi Delta Kappan*, 56, 670-677.

8. Gilligan, C. and J. Attanucci. "Two Moral Orientations: Gender Differences and Similarities." *Merrill Palmer Quarterly*, 34, 223-237.

Chapter 6

1. Binet, A. *L'Etude experimentale de L'intelligence*. Paris: Schleicher Freres, 1903.

2. Binet, A. and T. Simon."Methods Novelles pour le Diagnostic du Niveau Intellectual des Anormaux." *Annee Psychol.*, 11, 191-244.

3. Terman, L. *The Measurement of Intelligence*. Boston: Houghton Mifflin, 1916.

4. Wechsler, D. *Measurement of Adult Intelligence*. Baltimore: Williams & Wilkins, 1939.

5. Wechsler, D. *The Wechsler Intelligence Scale for Children, Revised*. New York: The Psychological Corporation, 1991.

6. Wechsler, D. *The Wechsler Preschool and Primary School Scale of Intelligence-R*. New York: The Psychological Corporation, 1987.

7. Spearman, C. *The Abilities of Man*. New York: Macmillan, 1927.

8. Thurstone, L. "Primary Mental Abilities." *Psychometric Monographs*, 1, 1939.

9. Guilford, J. "The Structure of Intellect." *Psychological Bulletin*, 53, 267-293.

10. Horn, J. *Psychometric Studies of Aging and Intelligence*. New York: Raven Press, 1975.

11. Sternberg, R. *The Triarchic Theory of the Mind*. New York: Viking Press, 1988.

12. Gardner, H. *Frames of Mind*. New York: Basic Books, 1983.

13. Clement, J. and L. Schweinhart, W. Barnett, A. Epstein, D. Weikart. *Changed Lives*. Ypsilanti, MI: High/Scope Educational Foundation, 1984.

14. Terman, L. and M. Oden. *Genetic Studies of Genius (Vol. 5)*. Stanford, CA: Stanford University Press, 1916.

15. Hollingsworth, L. and R. Kaunitz. "The Centile Status of Gifted Children at Maturity." *Journal of Genetic Psychology*, 45, 106-120.

16. Witty, P. "A Genetic Study of Fifty Gifted Children." In National Society for the Study of Eduation (Ed.), *Intelligence: Its Nature and Nurture*. Bloomington, IL: Public School Publishing, 1940.

17. Hildreth, G. "Three Gifted Children: A Developmental Study." *Journal of Genetic Psychology*, 85, 239-262.

18. Cox, J. and N. Daniel, N. Boston. *Educating Able Learners*. Austin, TX: University of Texas Press.

19. Hildreth, G. *Introduction to the Gifted*. New York: McGraw Hill, 1966.

20. Torrance, E. *Torrance Tests of Creative Thinking*. Bensenville, IL: Scholastic Testing Service, 1984.

21. Getzels, J. and P. Jackson. *Creativity and Intelligence*. New York: Wiley, 1962.

22. Ibid.

23. Hobson, J. "Mental Age as a Workable Criterion for School Admission." *Elementary School Journal*, 48, 312-321.

24. Worcester, D. *The Education of Children of Above Average Mentality*. Lincoln, NE: University of Nebraska Press, 1956.

Chapter 7

1. American Psychiatric Association. *Diagnostic and Statistical Manual of Mental Disorders (Third Ed. Rev.).* Washington, DC: American Psychiatric Association, 1994.
2. Elkind, D. *Child Development and Education.* New York: Oxford University Press, 1976.
3. American Psychiatric Association. *Op. cit.*
4. Kirk, S. and J. Gallagher. *Educating Exceptional Students.* Boston: Houghton Mifflin, 1989.
5. Weininger, O. *Time-In's.* In press, 1998.
6. Elkind, D. *Ties That Stress.* Cambridge, MA: Harvard University Prss, 1994.

Chapter 8

1. Baron, N. *Growing Up with Language.* Reading, MA: Addison Wesley, 1992.
2. Stoll, C. *Silicon Snake Oil.* New York: Doubleday, 1995.
3. Oppenheimer, T. "The Computer Delusion." *The Atlantic Monthly,* July, 1997, 45-62.
4. Papert, S. *The Children's Machine: Rethinking School in an Age of the Computer.* New York: Basic Books, 1993.
5. Healy, J. *Endangered Minds.* New York: Simon & Schuster, 1990.
6. Guthrie, L. and S. Richardson. "Language Arts: Computer Literacy in the Primary Grades." *Educational Leadership,* October, 1995, 53(2), 14-17.
7. Ginott, H. *Between Parent and Child.* New York: Avon, 1969.
8. Erikson, E. *Childhood and Society.* New York: Norton, 1950.
9. Turecki, S. *The Emotional Problems of Normal Children.* New York: Bantam Books, 1994.
10. Weininger, O. *Time-In's.* In press, 1998.

Index

A

Academic learners, reinventing young children as, 154-157
Acceleration, 126
Accommodative play, 24
Across-gender play, 108
Adaptation type as basis of temperament, 91-92
African-American children, teaching, 74
Age in learning second language, 53
Aggressiveness, 83-84
    gender differences in, 106
Alternative uses task, 124
Anal stage, 26
Articulation difficulties, 138-39
Assertiveness, 99
Assimilative play, 24
Attention Deficit/Hyperactivity Disorder (ADHD), 72, 144-145
Autoeroticism, 26
Autonomy, 14-15, 38

B

Babar books, 59
Baron, Naomi, 59, 158-159
Basal readers, ii, 57-58
Behavior disorders, 145-147
Bilingual education, 43, 55
Binet, Alfred, 112, 114, 116, 123
Birthday scripts, 79-80
Birth order differences, 88, 101-105

blended-family birth-order reversals, 104-105
    first-born children, 101
    last-born children, 102
    middle children, 101-102
    only children, 103
    variations in, 103
Black English, 43, 50
Blended-family birth-order reversals, 104-105
Blindness, 132
Body type as basis of temperament, 89-90
Books, reading, ii
Brazelton, T. Berry, 16
Brosterman, N., 21

C

Cambodian children, teaching, 73-74
Chess, S., 91
Child abuse, 7
Childhood
    disappearance of, i
    inventing and reinventing, 1-18
    modern invention of, 1
    reinventing, 153-71
Child psychiatry, Erikson's contributions to, 37-40
Child-rearing, being knowledgeable about, 6
Children. *See* Early childhood education; Young children
Chomsky, Noam, 45-46, 57
Chronological age, 113, 125-126

181

Classroom
  books in, ii
  learning rules for, 66-67
Colloquial expressions, 54-55
Communication, nonverbal, 60-62
Communication disorders, 138-139
Competence, 15-16
Computers
  and learning style, 97
  young children as educational
    users, 160-163
Concrete operations, 32
Consensual love, 13
Convergent thinking, 124
Creationism, 3
Crystalized intelligence, 116-117
Cultural values, gender differences
  in, 107
Culture
  language differences between,
    46-48
  language differences within,
    48-51
  and temperament, 92-95
Curriculum-disabled children, 74,
  143
  working with, 143-144
Curriculum frames, 65
Custodial children, 141

D

Darwin, Charles, 3, 99-100
Deafness, 132
Deaf voice, 137
Debussy, Claude, 128
de Tocqueville, A., 94
Developmentally appropriate
  practice, 173-174
Dewey, John, 163
Disciplinary scripts, 83-84
Discipline, 169-171
Divergent thinking, 124
Diversity, 108-109

Domain-specific issues, 11
Domesticity, 5, 6, 14
Dysfunctional frame behavior,
  78-79

E

Early childhood, iii-iv
  postmodern concept of, 16-17
Early childhood education
  Froebel's contributions to,
    20-21
  and gifted, 125-28
  and intelligence testing, 118-20
  and modern parenting, 9
  Montessori's contributions to,
    22-24
  Piaget's contributions to, 31-34
  and postmodern child-rearing,
    17
  Steiner's contributions to,
    28-31
  teaching reading in, 56-60
Ectomorphs, 89
Edison, Thomas, 160
Educable children, 140-141
Educational computer users, young
  children as, 160-163
Educational technology users, rein-
  venting young children as,
  157-163
Educational television viewers,
  young children as, 157-160
Educational toys, 23
Egocentrism, 31-32
Emotional needs, reinventing for
  young children, 163-171
Endomorph, 89-90
English
  Black, 43, 50
  Pidgin, 49-50
  as a second language, 51-56
  Standard, 49
Enlightenment, 2

Erikson, Erik, 19, 37-40, 165-166
Evolution, theory of, 3
Expressive disorders, 138-139
Externalization, 146
Extroverts, 90

F

Families
    blended, 104-5
    discipline in, 83-84
    modern nuclear, 3-7
    parenting scripts in, 84-85
    personal property in, 82-83
    postmodern permeable, 12-13
    traditional nuclear, 12-13
    vital, 174
Family romance, 26-27
Fernald School for the Blind, 132
Fine-motor coordination, gender
        differences in, 107
First born children, 101, 104, 105
Fixation, 25-26
Flesh, Rudolf, 57
Fluid intelligence, 116
Foul language scripts, 81-82
Frames, 64, 65-79
    clashes in, 72-75
    curriculum, 65
    modifying, 77-79
    people, 65
    rules for, 68, 71-72
    situational, 65
    spoiled, 68-72
    switches in, 75-76
    teaching, 66-68
    travel, 65
    variety of, 65-66
French children, temperament in, 93
Freud, Sigmund, 3, 8, 19, 25-28,
        112
Froebel, Freidrich, 8, 9, 17, 19,
        20-21

G

Galton, Sir Francis, 112
Gardner, Howard, 116, 117, 120
Gender differences, 88, 105-109
Genetic endowment, 122
Gershwin, George, 128
Gesell, Arnold, 44-45
Gestures, 61
Getzels, J., 124-25
Giftedness, 111, 120-128. *See also*
        Intelligence
    definition of, 111
    and early childhood education,
        125-128
    in the modern era, 120-123
    in the postmodern era, 123-125
Gilligan, Carol, 106
Ginott, Haim, 164
Goethe, Johann Wolfgang von, 123
Goffman, Erving, 64
Goodman, Kenneth, 57
Goodness of fit, 91-92
Gravity, laws of, 3
Guilford, J., 116, 120
Guilt, 39

H

Head Start programs, 73-74, 119,
        154
Healy, Jane, 162
Hearing impairment, 137-138
High Scope Organization, 119
Hildreth, G., 122
Hochschild, Arlie, 166
Hollingsworth, L., 122
Horn, John, 116, 120
Hunter College, 126
Hyperactive-impulsive children,
        144-145
Hypertext, 161

I

Illness scripts, 80-81
I messages, 164
Immigrant families, children in, 6-7
Impulsiveness, 97-98
Inattentive children, 144
Inclusion, 126-127, 136, 155
    developing successful strate-
        gies in, 148-150
Individuals with Disabilities in Edu-
    cation Act, 135, 136
Industry, 40
Infantile sexuality, 3
Inferiority, 40, 106
Initiative, 39
Innocence of children, 6
Intelligence, 111-120. *See also* Gift-
    edness
    definition of, 111
    in the modern era, 111-114
    in the postmodern era, 111,
        114-117
Intelligence Quotient (IQ), 114,
    140-141
Intelligence testing, and early child-
    hood education, 118-120
Internalization, 145-146
Interpersonal interaction, 162-163
Introverts, 90

J

Jackson, P., 124-125
Japanese children, temperament in,
    93, 94

K

Kagan, Jerome, 97
Kaunitz, R., 122
Kindergarten, 9, 20-21, 118
    early admittance to, 125, 126
Kohlberg, Lawrence, 106

L

Language, 11
    foul, scripts, 81-82
    receptive, 139
    supportive, 165
    Vygotsky on origin of, 35-36
Language development, 43-62
    from modern to postmodern,
        44-46
    non-verbal communication in,
        60-62
    Piaget on, 31-32
Language differences
    between cultures, 46-48
    within cultures, 48-51
Language experience approach to
    reading, 57-58
Last born children, 102, 104, 105
Latency stage, 27
Leach, Penelope, 16
Learning disabilities, 141-145
    working with, 143-144
Learning styles, 88, 95-100
    personality-linked, 97-100
    sensory, 96-97
Least restrictive environment,
    135-136
Lennenburg, Eric, 53
Leveling, 100
Logo program, 161
Love
    consensual, 13
    maternal, 4-5, 6
    romantic, 4, 5-6, 7
Lumpers, 99-100

M

Magical thinking, 165
Mainstreaming, 135
Manners, 66
Manual group on hearing impair-
    ment, 137

Maternal instinct, 6
Maternal love, 4-5, 6
Math skills, gender differences in, 106
Mediated learning experience, 161
Mediation, 35
Mental age, 113, 125-126
Mentally ill, 111-112
Mentally limited, 111-112
Mental retardation, 118, 139-141
Mesomorphs, 89
Middle children, 101-2, 104, 105
Modern childhood, 7-9
Modern era
    giftedness in, 120-123
    intelligence in, 111-114
Modern nuclear family, 3-4
    sentiments of, 4-7
Modern world view, 2-9
Montessori, Maria, 8, 9, 17, 19, 21, 22-24, 25, 27, 28, 37-38, 59, 118-119, 160, 162, 169
Moral development, stages of, 106
Motivation
    in learning oral language, 58
    in learning second language, 53-54
Mount Hope School (Rochester, N.Y.), 143
Mozart, Wolfgang Amadeus, 120-121
Mr. Rogers' Neighborhood, 157-160
Multi-age groupings, 156-157
Multi-cultural curricula, 17
Multiple intelligences, 117

N

National Association for Retarded Children, 134
Native American children, learning style of, 99
Navaho children, teaching, 73

Need imbalance, i
Newton, Sir Isaac, 3
New York State Cerebral Palsy Association, 134
Nietzsche, F., 11
Non-verbal communication, 60-62
Normality, 131-151
Nursery schools, 9

O

Oedipus complex, 3, 26, 27, 28
Omote, 93
Only children, 103
Oppenheimer, Todd, 161, 162
Oral group on hearing impairment, 137
Oral language, gender differences in, 107
Oral stage, 25-26
Overprotectiveness of children, 6

P

Papert, Seymour, 161
Parent-child interactions, 166-169
Parenting, modern, and early childhood education, 9
Parenting scripts, 84-85
Parent organizations, and recognition of special needs children, 134
Passivity, 99
People frames, 65
Perception
    of social roles, 63-64
    of special needs, 132-137
Performance, 120
Performance scales, 114-115
Personality, 87-109
    birth order differences in, 88, 101-105
    gender differences in, 88, 105-109
    learning styles in, 88, 95-100

Personality (*cont'd*)
temperament in, 87-88, 88-95
Personality-linked learning styles, 97-100
Personal property scripts, 82-83
Pestalozzi, Johan Heinrich, 20
Piaget, Jean, 8, 19, 31-34, 45, 53, 113, 126, 140-141, 162
Pidgin English, 49-50
Play
accommodative, 24
across-gender, 108
assimilative, 24
Point scale of intelligence, 114
Portfolios, 120
Postmodern child-rearing, and early childhood education, 17
Postmodern era
early childhood in, 16-17
giftedness in, 123-125
intelligence in, 111, 114-117
Postmodern permeable family, 12-13
sentiments of, 13-15
Postmodern society, negative consequences of transition into, i-ii
Postmodern world view, 10-17
Preoperational thinking, 32
Prepared environment, 23
Preschool children, learning disabilities in, 142
Preschool environment, sensory-oriented, 136
Progress, belief in human, 2
Projects, 120
Psychology, contributions of Vygotsky to, 34-37
Psychosexual development
Erikson on, 165-166
Freud on, 25-28
Public Law 94-142, 135
Pull-out programs, 126

Q

Quality time, 163, 166-67

R

Reading
books, ii
language experience approach to, 57-58
teaching, to young children, 56-60
whole word approach to, 59-60
Recapituation theory, 44
Receptive disorders, 138-139
Receptive language, 139
Reflectiveness, 98
Regularity, 2
Reinvention, 153
Resource specialists, availability of, 150
Retention, 155
Rifkin, Jeremy, 166
Role differentiation, commitment to, 4
Romantic idealism, 4
Romantic love, 4, 5-6, 7
Rousseau, Henri, 20, 173
Rukun, 92-93

S

Satanic possession, 3
Scripts, 64, 79-85
birthday, 79-80
disciplinary, 83-84
foul language, 81-82
illness, 80-81
parenting, 84-85
personal property, 82-83
Second language, English as a, 51-56
Self-esteem, 163, 168
reinventing children's, 164-166
Self-worth, 168

Sensory disabilities, 137-138
Sensory learning styles, 96-97
Sensory-oriented preschool envi-
    ronment, 136
Service work, 14
Sesame Street, 154, 157-160
Sex typing, 107
Shame, 38
Shared parenting, 13-14
Sharpening, 100
Sheldon, William, 89-90
Sight words, 59-60
Simon, Theodore, 112-113
Situational frame, 65
Skinner, B. F., 160
Slang, 54-55
Slips of the tongue, 3
Smith, Frank, 57
Social invention and reinvention,
    1-2
Socialization, 63-86
    frames in, 65-79
    scripts in, 79-85
Social needs, reinventing for young
    children, 163-171
Social orientation as basis of tem-
    perament, 90
Social roles
    concept of, 63
    perception of, 63-64
Spatial abilities, gender differences
    in, 107
Spearman, Charles, 116
Special needs, perceptions of,
    132-137
Special schools for the gifted, 126
Splitters, 100
Spoiled frames, 68-72
Spousal abuse, 7
Stammering, 139
Standard English, 49
Stanford-Binet intelligence test,
    113-114, 121-23

Steiner, 34
Stern, William, 113-114
Sternberg, Robert, 116, 117
Stoll, Clifford, 159-160
Stranger anxiety, 108
Strenberg, R., 120
Stuttering, 138, 139
Sub-languages, 49-50
Superiority, 106
Supportive language, 165
Symbolic learning experience, 161

T

Taylor, A. R., 8
Teacher-to-child ratio, 148
Temperament, 87-88, 88-95
    adaptation type as basis of,
        91-92
    body type as basis of, 89-90
    and culture, 92-95
    social orientation as basis of,
        90
Terman, Lewis, 113-114, 121-123
Thomas, A., 91
Thurstone, L., 116, 120
Time-in, 147, 170-171
Time-limit metaphors, 76
Time-outs, 147, 163, 169-171
Togetherness, 5-6
Total communication, 137
Traditional nuclear family, 12-13
Trainable children, 140-141
Transductive thinking, 32
Transition class, 155-156
Travel frames, 65
Triarchic theory of intelligence, 117
Tutors, 144

U

Universality, 2
Ura, 93
Urbanity, 14

V

Verbal scales, 114-115
Virginity, 4
Virtual reality, 162
Visual impairment, 138
Vital families, 174
Vital teaching, 173-174
Vygotsky, Lev, 19, 34-37

W

Waldorf Schools, 28
Wechsler, David, 114, 120
Wechsler Scales, 114-116
Weininger, Otto, 147, 170-171
Whole word approach to reading,
    59-60
WISC, 115-116
WISC-R, 115-116
Wittgenstein, L., 11
Witty, 122
World view
    modern, 2-9

postmodern, 10-17
WPPSI, 115-116
WPPSI-R, 115-116
Writing problems, children with,
    142

Y

You messages, 164
Young children
    reinventing, as academic learn-
        ers, 154-157
    reinventing, as educational
        technology users, 157-163
    reinventing self-esteem for,
        164-166
    reinventing social and emo-
        tional needs of, 163-171
    teaching reading to, 56-60

Z

Zone of proximal development, 36